AWAKENING A WOMAN'S SOUL

The Power of Meditation and
Mindfulness to Transform Your Life

BEV JANISCH

Bev Janisch Publishing
www.bevjanisch.com

ISBN
978-1-9995694-1-9 (Hardcover)
978-1-9995694-0-2 (Paperback)
978-1-9995694-3-3 (EPUB)
978-1-9995694-2-6 (MOBI)

**To my grandchildren, Johnny and Brooklyn,
and all the little Souls to come after you.**

May you always use your head in service of your heart.
May you create space for your Soul and honor what you hear.
May you love yourself, just as you are.

*May you always remember that there is a life
force that is expressed through you.*

Table of Contents

And the day came when the risk to remain tight in a bud was more painful than the risk it took to blossom.

— *Anais Nin*

Introduction

We are at a time in the evolution of our planet when many women are experiencing an inner pull and urge to give birth to a new way of being. Women of all ages are asking deeper questions about the purpose and meaning of our lives. We feel a need to fully express ourselves in a way that nourishes our Souls. This shift from being outwardly driven by material and traditional definitions of success to being inspired by our Souls, is causing inner earthquakes in many of us that may be confusing and misunderstood. We are shattering many of our long-held beliefs about what it means to be a woman and how we show up for ourselves and in our relationships. We are being called to undergo a deep and lasting transformation that reflects a shift from family and societal conditioning and expectations to a higher expression of our deepest truths based on the needs of our Souls. We are becoming increasingly aware of this inner urge, which has many of us wondering: *How do I let go of who I think I should be to step fully into who I am?*

This book is about how to live a life that is in service of our highest and most Essential Self—our Soul. It's about learning how to *be* different and not just *do* different. It is for women who are ready for a transformation, who are being called to "something" new. You may not know what this looks like, but you have an intuitive knowing that the "something" is inside of you. You may also have a sense that this inner "something" is calling to you and that it needs you to listen. Perhaps you're searching for inner peace and a grounding that will keep you steady during the inevitable storms in your life. Maybe you have a desire to feel deeply connected and seen in your relationships. Perhaps you're ready to let go of the "should" in your life and live in alignment with what brings you alive and sparks that joy inside of you. You may have a longing for deeper meaning or purpose. Whatever your "something" is, you are meant to listen.

It seems that women of all ages feel something is missing in our lives. This inner restlessness and longing does not mean we're depressed, and a pill won't solve it. We're not broken, wounded or dysfunctional. Instead, it means we're being called to break through to greater inner peace, vitality and happiness. It means our Souls are speaking to us and inviting us to learn about a new way of being. It means we need to pause and look at our lives. Ultimately, it means that somewhere along the way and in the midst of our busy lives, we've lost touch with the truth of who we are, and we are being called to awaken our Souls.

What I've learned from working with women is that many of us struggle with the same question: "How shall I live that enables me to thrive and feel deeply connected and fulfilled in my life?" I've learned that many of us don't just want to fill our days and feel like we're sleepwalking through life. We want to feel deeply alive, experience vibrant health and meaningful relationships, and know that our lives matter. We want to be open to life and to feel grounded so that we don't fall over or get thrown off balance when we face inevitable challenges.

I've had the privilege of working with hundreds of women through meditation workshops and individual mentoring. I've found that women are hungry for change and creating new ways of being. We don't want to *do* more we want to *be* more.

A number of years ago, I was lost and confused and couldn't understand what my inner tension and restlessness was all about. My health was beginning to suffer, and I was feeling as if my life lacked meaning, depth, and vitality. The feeling of living fully had become buried beneath my roles and self-imposed expectations of what it meant to be a good woman and a worthy human being. I felt confused because I had so much to feel grateful for. I was living the dream! This confusion was intermingled with guilt for feeling the way I did. I found myself asking: *What could I be missing in the midst of an abundant and fortunate life?*

I'd had a long, fulfilling career as a nurse; I was married to a great guy, who happened to be my high school sweetheart; I had a great relationship with my adult children and their spouses; and I had amazing friends and family. What I came to learn was that "I" was missing.

I had no idea who I was at the core of my being or how to go about finding the Self I had lost in my societal roles when I had unknowingly bought into the beliefs about what it meant to be a woman. Many of us look outside ourselves for the answers that can only be found within. Where do you begin to look when you don't know who you are and you have no idea what could possibly be wrong in your life?

For me, it was numerous synchronistic events and signs from the "universe" that led me to explore and experience meditation, mindfulness, and the wisdom teachings. This inner exploration and adventure were part of my Soul's journey and evolution. It's also part of my calling to share with you what I have learned, struggled with, overcome, experienced, and transformed along the way to connecting with my Soul. While most of my past writing has been from an academic perspective, I was meant to write this book about my personal experience from a place of vulnerability. I share my Soul with you, along with the stories of a number of inspiring women with whom I have journeyed. Our ages, stories and life circumstances are all different, but the underlying pull to awaken our Souls has been the common thread. There was something in each of us that called us to wake up, shed our limiting beliefs, and begin to live fully.

To honor anonymity, I have changed the women's names and identifying details, and in some cases I have combined more than one story together. This was easy to do, as I realized that while the women are all very different, the challenges and struggles we experience are similar. Their stories are inspiring and demonstrate how inner exploration and growth can create a context to shine brighter in this world. They bring hope that transformation and greater inner peace and fulfillment are possible.

It's important for you to know that while these women were committed to change and creating new ways of "being," they weren't committed to silent retreats, sitting for more than a few minutes in meditation, sitting cross-legged on the floor, changing their spiritual beliefs or being meditation "junkies." They wove simple practices into their already busy lives. They were stay-at-home moms, corporate business leaders, doctors, nurses, and receptionists who listened to the call of their Souls to return home to themselves and begin thriving in their lives.

As you reflect on the stories, wisdom, and Soul practices being shared in this book, I hope you will see and feel that you are not alone in facing some of the challenges so many of us have in our lives. This book is intended to spark insights in you that will help you connect with your Self and get to know that Self, perhaps for the very first time. While this book refers to different meditation and mindfulness practices, it is not a *how to meditate* book. Rather, it aims to focus on how the practices help create an inner landscape that enables you to become a whole and thriving human being who has united your Soul with all aspects of your life, including your roles.

This book is about awakening your Soul. It's about becoming aware and letting go of limiting beliefs, and it's about shifting from being externally motivated to please and satisfy others to being internally motivated by your Soul. Even though you may not know exactly what the Soul is, you know at some deep level that there is something in you wanting to wake up and be expressed through you.

During this journey to connect with your Soul, you will have a number of dragons to slay. These dragons happen to be our beliefs—or more accurately, our misbeliefs. We'll challenge many of our beliefs about what it means to be a good woman in the fulfillment of our roles in relationships, vocations, and lives. We'll explore the inner power struggle that exists between success—as defined by widely held cultural beliefs—and the Soul's desire for meaning and purpose and to live more deeply. We'll uncover the ways of being in our relationships that are based on an outdated relationship model that leaves our Soul hungry for a deeper connection. We'll gain an awareness of the impact that our conditioned beliefs have over our current lives and learn why our Souls rebel. We'll learn how to tap into our intuition in order to bring our life back into alignment with an intelligent life force and our deepest truths.

Throughout this book you'll gain practical tools to shift your way of being from one that feels constricted and fearful to one that is expanded and free. You will learn how to feel settled inside even when things around you are in chaos. You'll develop the capacity to deal with your feelings and all the stories that you tell yourself. You'll discover what it means to be self-compassionate and how to love yourself unconditionally. You'll experience what it feels like to forgive and let go of anger, resentment, and disappointment. You'll know what it means to follow your heart and tap into inner wisdom. And finally, you'll begin to take steps to bring your life back into alignment with the longings of your Soul.

At the end of each chapter, we'll explore the misbeliefs held by many women that keep us disconnected from our Souls—powerful beliefs that have defined our sense of Self in a way that prevents us from thriving in our lives. We'll then embark on simple practices or reflections to help you awaken your Soul. In addition to these end-of-chapter practices, there are additional practices instrumental in my own life that I have outlined at the end of the book.

If you are being summoned to listen to the whisperings of your Soul, you will be joining a community of women who are answering the call to grow and evolve, and who are seeking and open to new ways of being. Women who have an inner urge and desire to bring everything in their life into alignment with the wisdom of their Soul, and who are willing to dive deep to retrieve the pearls at the bottom of the sea.

My own journey began a few years ago as I was preparing to climb one of the highest mountains in the world, Mount Kilimanjaro.

CHAPTER 1

In Search of Your Soul

I came to realize that my happiness would be found by going deeper rather than higher. Going higher just took me further away from my Soul.

—Bev Janisch

It's a universal truth that most disruptions in life come at the most inopportune times. A month before I was to set out on the biggest adventure of my life, I found myself sitting in a therapist's office saying, "I have so much in my life to feel grateful for, and yet I feel that something is missing. I feel empty inside and I've lost my way. I've been married for thirty years to my high school sweetheart and although we spend a lot of time together, I feel really disconnected from him. I love him, but sometimes I feel like we're just roommates. I'm living the dream and I have no idea why I'm not happier. It's not that I'm depressed, I'm just feeling like something is missing and I have no idea how to figure it out."

I had a sense of urgency because in a few weeks I'd be travelling to Africa with my husband, Mark, to climb Mount Kilimanjaro. Through the tears that I was desperately trying to hold in, I told the therapist "I feel like an emotional wreck and I'm supposed to be so excited for this trip of a lifetime." I left her office that day realizing that when I returned from

Africa I would be taking a different journey, one that traditional therapy or counseling couldn't "fix." I had no idea what the journey would be, why I needed to take it, or how I would embark on it when I returned from Africa.

In the year leading up to the trek, I prepared myself in every way possible to ensure I would make it to the top. I signed up for *Fit for Trips*, a company that gave me an individualized fitness plan to ensure I would be physically ready. I spent hours going up and down stairs in my backyard with books in my backpack, sometimes taking three steps at a time. I spent countless hours on the treadmill set at a steep incline to get me ready for the climb. I lifted weights and took a step-by-step approach to get myself ready, rarely missing a day. I knew that many people didn't reach the top because of the altitude rather than their fitness level, but I wanted to create every opportunity for success.

As the trip approached, I noticed that I was getting increasingly anxious. I had downloaded numerous books to get pointers about what to bring and what I would need on the mountain. I had talked to people who had done it, researched the medications I needed to bring, had a list I'd checked countless times, and even found the best solar charger I could get my hands on because god forbid I wouldn't be able to listen to my audiobooks to calm me down or provide a distraction. There was a growing realization that all the physical preparation and information gathering wasn't going to prepare me to be emotionally resilient and cope with the fear that was creeping in about climbing a mountain. I had no idea how to prepare mentally for this adventure and that scared me to death. This trip was beginning to shine a glimmer of awareness on the fact that I had never learnt how to deal with uncomfortable feelings. I also knew I was running out of time, but even if I had more time, I didn't know how to become emotionally stronger and more resilient. I downloaded two audiobooks I thought might help me if I began freaking out while we were away: *The Power of Now* by Eckhart Tolle, and *Meditation for Beginners* by Jack Kornfield.

Mark, while trying to be supportive, thought I was crazy. He couldn't understand why it was such a big deal and why I felt I needed to prepare so much. This really ticked me off, because I kept thinking, *You got me into this mess and I'm really doing this because you want to, and you can't even be bothered to spend time training with me.* I also knew that although it appeared that we had the perfect relationship, I felt disconnected from him and didn't know how to share my feelings so I could feel seen and heard. Truth be told, my inner restlessness and a feeling that something was missing had been going on for a number of years.

Mark and I had retired young and after the initial feeling of freedom and the enjoyment of lots of amazing trips wore off, I felt completely empty. I knew something needed to change but didn't know what. I had been a successful nurse, working first with people with dementia and then later in my career with people needing palliative care. I had two grown children who were successfully launched, I had amazing family and friends, and yet still I felt like something was missing. I felt empty inside, but I had no idea how to connect with my deeper Self in order to shed some light on what was contributing to this feeling.

With a heavy heart and a sense of confusion, I boarded our plane with Mark one snowy, cold morning in January. As I embarked on the journey to climb to one of the highest spots on the planet, I had never felt lower.

We arrived in Africa and met up with our trekking companions. It was January 6, 2013 and my horoscope for the day read, "Do something different today because you're hungry for adventure and you want to learn something new. At the very least, take a different route travelling to or from somewhere. Read something different. Try an ethnic restaurant. Shake it up a little." Boy, was I about to shake it up a little. I was about to shake it up a *lot*. What I didn't realize at the time was that I was hungry to meet the needs of my Soul, not needing a physical challenge that could be satisfied by climbing a mountain. It was hunger of a different nature, one that I didn't know existed: *Soul hunger.*

Mark and I spent the next couple of days getting to know the others in our group and preparing for the start of our trek. The night before we started our climb, I made a note in my journal: "It's 4 am and I am fully awake—must be jet lag that is kicking in. It's hard not to let my mind wander to the upcoming hike, so I keep reminding myself to *be in the moment.*" I guess that was part of my problem. I had no idea how to *be in the moment.*

The next morning before we set off for the hike, I made another note in my journal about my hiking companions. I noticed that they were "nice people, and that it's interesting to me how some people are more laid back and seem to worry less. I definitely seem to be the worry wart." I then made a note that "I need to practice worrying less." Along with my Einstein realization about learning to *live in the moment*, how on earth was I supposed to learn how to worry less? I definitely had more questions than answers.

After the first couple of days on the mountain, we seemed to get into a routine. We got used to living and sleeping in tents with limited space, and the days on the mountain were full and thrilling, which meant I never had an opportunity to feel my emptiness. The nights, on the other hand, were long and cold. Mark and I would crawl into our tents every night at about seven as the sun was going down and the temperatures were dropping. After getting myself mummified in the sleeping bag and set up for the night, I would grab my iPhone and begin listening to stories to distract myself from my aching Soul and the fear of the unknown.

A few days into our trek we arrived at camp after a long day of trekking that had taken us higher and higher up the mountain. We rounded a corner and there, nestled in a lush valley in the mountain, was the camp where we would spend the night. My feet were tired and aching from a long day, and since it was our fifth day on the trek, I was beginning to feel weary. Beside our campsite there was a stream that created such a soothing sound that it brought an inner peace. In an attempt to ease my aching feet, I decided to remove my boots and socks and put my feet in the mountain stream. A sense of gratitude enveloped me as I did so, and I felt all my weariness fading away as the water soothed not only my feet but also my Soul. A deep feeling of inner contentment settled over me as I listened to the birds chirping and the soft sounds of the flowing water. To this day, I remember every sensation that flowed through my mind and body as I thought to myself, *so this is what it feels like to live in the moment and be fully alive.*

Those few minutes of sitting with my feet in that stream showed me what I had been missing out on in my life—the ability to pay attention and fully, completely enjoy the simple moments. My mind was free of worrying about what might happen as we got higher on the mountain and the altitude kicked in, and I knew I wanted and needed to learn how to create more moments like that in my life.

The final night on the mountain was spent sleeping in the crater at around 18,000 feet above sea level. We had reached the summit in mid afternoon and after a brief celebration, we started the short but snowy, steep hike down into the crater. At this point, we were all completely exhausted.

Every step was an effort. The nights had all been long, but that night was longer than most. Icy rain pelted down on our tent and we had every layer of clothing on trying to stay warm. One woman in our group was taken down to lower elevations that night as she was showing signs of altitude sickness. I could feel the fear settling in, combined with a sense of relief that it was our last night on the mountain. After a sleepless night, and many trips out of the tent to pee (because the altitude drugs are a diuretic that make you pee more often), I decided to use my little contraption that makes it possible for women to pee in a bottle. I was pretty proud of myself because I did it without peeing all over my sleeping bag.

In the morning when I went to empty it, however, I realized I had peed in my water bottle. That minor thing, combined with major sleep deprivation and exhaustion, set me off. I was in tears as I struggled to put on my mittens and prepare for the long trek down. I turned to Mark, who had noticed I was crying, and said, "Can you help me put my mittens on?" He smiled and said, "Of course."

Looking back, I realize I had never learned how to ask for help. I had believed that asking for help was a sign of weakness. I also didn't expect to be comforted or to get a hug when I was feeling scared. And even more puzzling, I wasn't aware that I didn't know how to be vulnerable or that these beliefs were starving my Soul. Over the years, I had just shut down and lost my Self in my marriage and a life that was lived based on how things "should" be. I knew Mark was a great guy, but I had blamed him for the fact that I had been feeling lost and a bit confused in my life. I could feel a sense of anger and resentment always simmering under the surface, like a volcano ready to erupt. I thought if I fixed my marriage, I'd be happier. But I had no idea my journey was going to be about healing and rediscovering my Self.

As we got to the bottom of the mountain on a drizzling, muddy day in January, I was about to embark on a journey to reconnect with the parts of myself that I had lost or had been buried over the years. I had no way of knowing that the changes would be profound and impact every part of my life. I was about to say "hello" to my Soul for the first time and get to know parts of myself that I didn't know existed. It was the beginning of a journey to learn that there was much more to "me" than I had ever thought possible.

Say "Hello" to Your Soul

On the journey towards awakening our Soul, one of our greatest challenges is getting to know the two parts that make up our sense of Self. Becoming aware is incredibly powerful because it means that we can choose which part of our Self we're going to listen to and ultimately align our lives with. We all have a Small Self and a Soul. The Small Self, commonly referred to as our ego, is concerned with keeping us safe and in our comfort zones. When we're living from our Small Self, we are largely living our lives based on preprogrammed beliefs about who we should become and how we should behave. We are living from a place of fear where our primary focus is on safety and having our basic needs met. We are often in relationships with others because it feels comfortable and we're expecting that they will complete us. The Small Self thrives on judgment, comparison, and a sense of never being good enough.

The Small Self also tells us that the more we have in terms of "things," the happier we will be. It leaves us believing that happiness is just around the corner and when we have more money, a better job, relationship or vacation that we'll be happy. The Small Self is at war with the present moment and thrives when we focus on the past or the future. The Small Self shows up in either an overinflated sense of self or an underinflated one, which keeps us small, quiet, and in fear. Our Small Self doesn't want to acknowledge there's a higher intelligence at play in our lives. It believes we have control over everything and everyone. When our Small Self is running the show, we're living in our heads and disconnected from our hearts, intuition, and a deeper level of knowing.

Our Soul or Essential Self, on the other hand, is the truth of who we are. I call it "Essential" because it is essential that we connect with it and align our lives with it if we want to thrive in our physical, emotional, and spiritual well-being. It is a divine gift we're born with from an intelligence that exists within the universe. It's our blueprint for who we are at our core and contains the programming for who we're meant to become. When we make choices in our lives that are in service of our Soul, we begin to know and feel that we are living in alignment with our truths. We feel authentic.

The Soul thrives on freedom, expansion, growth, and self-expression. Its main desire is not to *achieve* more, but rather to *become* more. Your Soul is shy and will only reveal itself to you in the quiet moments when you are alone with yourself. Your connection with your Soul happens when you are fully present and engaged in the moment. While not physical in nature, your Soul can manifest itself with physical symptoms when you're not living in alignment with its intention.

Your Soul is always urging you to express yourself and live your life based on expansion, love, intuition, creativity, and flow.

The Soul and the Small Self are both part of who we are, but unfortunately, they often have a dysfunctional relationship. When we allow our Small Self to take the lead in our lives, our Soul has no choice but to rebel. With the Small Self driving the bus, we are never going to be heading in the right direction. We will continually get lost and will wonder why our life feels like it's lacking something and off course.

What most people don't realize is that we need to see our Small Self for what it is and then ask it to move to the back of the bus so that our Soul can take over driving. It's not that we're kicking the Small Self off the bus. That would be impossible because it's an important part of who we are. Rather, we just need to be kind as we ask it to move seats. Unfortunately, the message most of us receive on the path to living a Soul-based life is that our Small Self is "bad" and our Soul is "good." This message is coming from the Small Self and only serves to strengthen its hold on us. Accepting that we all have both a Small Self and a Soul enables us to live in harmony with who we are. When we give up the battle that is going on inside of us between our Small Self and our Soul we learn to listen, with wisdom, kindness, and grace.

There are a number of common signs that begin to surface in women's lives when our Souls are trying to get our attention:

- You realize that all the material things and ways that you are trying to fill yourself up aren't satisfying you. You're getting a sense that greater joy and fulfillment will not be gained by more wealth, exotic trips, having a nicer car or a bigger house. While you appreciate and enjoy these comforts, they do not define you.
- You feel a gap between who you are and how you're living and who you're meant to become and how you're meant to live.

- You have a feeling that something needs to be expressed through you. It's an inner urge that stems from deep within you. Ignoring the urge leaves you feeling divided or out of alignment.
- You realize that while your roles are important, you have a desire to not be defined by them. You may be asking, "who am I" and "what is my purpose?"
- You long for meaningful relationships that feel authentic, where you can feel accepted when the truth of who you are is expressed.
- You have a sense that some things need to change and fall away in order for your Soul to emerge. It may be relationships, work that you are doing, limiting beliefs, or how you fill your time.
- You are open to and curious about deepening your connection with something greater than yourself. You begin to realize that there are spiritual laws at work even if you don't know exactly how to tap into them.
- You notice that your values are shifting and new ones want to emerge. You have a sense that this shift will result in a new way of being and a rearranging of your priorities.
- You may feel a sense of discomfort as you're drawn into the unknown without a clear idea about how this process is meant to unfold.
- You have a desire to live in alignment with your Soul even though you don't have a picture of what that looks like.

While more and more women are experiencing this inner urge to undergo this transformation and be guided by our Soul, it's a relatively new shift in the evolution of our consciousness and therefore very confusing for many women. This shift is occurring as women challenge many of the beliefs that we had come to believe were true, such as the idea that material abundance will bring us happiness and fulfillment. We are increasingly looking for the deeper meaning of life and viewing ourselves as spiritual beings having a human experience. This inner urge is calling us to heal the parts of ourselves that keep us removed from our Souls so that we may thrive in both our human and spiritual lives. Because of this, I see countless women who have no idea what is going on inside of them, how to make sense of their inner restlessness, or what to do to move forward.

This shift is part of an evolutionary process that represents a dramatic change in where our sense of Self arises from. While many in society derive their identity from either victimhood, who they associate with, accomplishments, and status, women who are awakening derive their sense of Self from doing their inner work to heal and let go of what's holding them back in order to serve humanity in some way. The service I am referring to doesn't have to be some big, lofty thing; rather, it's the realization we're all connected in some way, and as we heal our own lives we create a ripple that extends out and emanates from us.

The awakening woman appreciates and is grateful for the comfort, freedom, and space provided by abundance, but she isn't defined by it.

This shift into a way of being that isn't the norm or fully understood brings certain challenges. Many women are confused by it and can't understand why it feels like something is missing when they have so much to feel grateful for. As we shift and embrace this realization and bring our lives into alignment with our deepest truths, it can feel very uncomfortable. We have never learned how to listen to our Souls, let alone live in alignment with them. As a result, many women don't listen or pay attention to these signs and then the longings of the Soul turn into what I call *Soul hunger*. If ignored long enough, it becomes full-on *Soul pain*.

The Soul Pain and Soul Hunger Wake-Up Call

For many years I worked as a palliative care nurse. There is no job on earth that is a greater privilege than being with people as they leave this physical world. I think what I loved the most about it and what made it such an honor, was the vulnerability and authenticity that death brings. It is raw, and real, and it highlights what matters most in this world. I bore witness to the suffering of the Soul that happens as people said goodbye to loved ones as their lives neared the end. This type of Soul pain made sense to me because who wouldn't have Soul pain as they think about what it means to die and leave everything and everyone that we've come to love.

But it was the Soul pain that was showing up in people who were not aware that they were dying and were very much engaged in the process of living that stumped me. While I haven't done palliative care for a number of years, I have seen a suffering of the Soul that happens in the context of living "healthy" lives. This suffering that I first experienced in my own life and bore witness to in the lives of women that I taught and mentored, confused me. As I was going through this suffering of the Soul, I really had no idea what it was and most importantly what it meant. It felt like an inner longing, aching, and restlessness that was always there. It was as if I was looking for something I knew was missing and out of my grasp, and yet I had no idea what it was. It was a yearning and feeling that something needed to burst out but couldn't. As one client said, "It felt like a split between who I was and who I was meant to become. It was like I was living a double life. The life I thought I should be living and the life I was being pulled to live. I felt like I needed a bridge and yet I didn't have one and had no idea how to build it."

I knew there was wisdom in this Soul hunger and pain. As a palliative care nurse, part of my job was to manage people's symptoms like pain, nausea, discomfort etc. The goal was to address and, where possible, remove the underlying causes for the symptom. When that wasn't possible, the focus was on measures to create greater comfort. We had effective medications that we could use to manage the symptoms even when we weren't able to "cure" the underlying illness or disease. But we always asked, "What is the nature of the pain or symptom, and what is causing it?"

I've come to view Soul pain in the same way. It is there for a reason, but unlike palliative symptoms, we are not meant to treat the symptoms. We are meant to get to the underlying cause, and to do that, we must first understand its nature. In this book, I share about Soul pain from my firsthand experience with it and from the themes that I see from working with many other women who also had it.

Soul pain feels like something is missing even though we have so much to feel grateful for. It feels like an inner aching or yearning that might dissipate for short periods of time but is usually there just beneath the surface. It looks like nothing on the outside and everything on the inside. It feels as if something needs to come through us, but we can't put our finger on it. It feels like emptiness and a misalignment between our roles and our Souls. It feels uncomfortable and confusing and hard to explain and articulate. It feels like a desire to burst out, grow, and expand while simultaneously confusing us because we don't know what that means. Soul pain is a trickster because it may show up like anxiety, depression, sleeplessness, inner stress, and health troubles.

I know from experience that Soul pain is manifested in physical and emotional symptoms and treating the physical symptom at the level of our biology is not going to address it. Many women I've worked with have been treated with antidepressants for the Soul pain they experience while living lives that aren't in alignment with their highest Self. No medication is ever going to fix that. That's not to say there is never a role for antidepressants or sleeping pills or any other measure to help deal with the discomfort. But using these measures to mask or numb the Soul pain isn't the answer. I view Soul pain as a gift from the universe. It's a call to wake up and figure out what is out of alignment in our life. We owe it to ourselves and to those in our lives to do the work, turn towards our Soul pain, and make some shifts.

Soul pain happens when we are living lives that are "two faced." Meaning that on one hand, we are living our lives based on conditioning, beliefs, what we should be doing, feeling etc.; and on the other hand, we have our inner Soul which is our blueprint from the divine and which has coded in us who we are meant to be. Just like an acorn is meant to be an oak tree, we are meant to be something. When these two faces don't line up, we have Soul pain. We are living divided lives and Soul pain is the symptom.

When our Soul is hungry or in pain, it can feel very lonely. Where do you go for your Soul pain? I went to a therapist, even though I knew I was mentally strong and resilient and didn't have mental health problems. I didn't want or need to be diagnosed, treated, fixed, or viewed as dysfunctional. I was highly functioning; I just had Soul pain. I went to a doctor who helped me manage my hormones, which were also a result of my Soul pain. Yet, the treatment I received from my doctor wasn't getting to the root of the problem, which I had yet to discover was the inner conflict that arose between my Small Self with all its distorted beliefs and my Soul, with an inner wisdom and the truth about who I was. Looking back, I can see now that I was aimlessly wandering and seeking help for my Soul pain.

To begin to understand this phenomenon that I had felt in my own life and that I'm seeing more often in women, I got curious. Since we are spiritual beings having a human experience, I wondered how Soul hunger compares to physical hunger. Physical hunger is described by words such as: *craving, desire, longing, urge, yearning, ache, emptiness, void, urge, vacancy, empty, lacking,* and *want* to name just a few. It became eerily familiar to me when I realized that these same words were what I heard daily from women who were by no means experiencing physical hunger. They were experiencing a hunger that was described in the same way but was from the Soul and not physical in nature.

I then turned to Google to explore phrases that people used when they described a sense of physical hunger:

- My energy would desert me, and weakness would take over.
- I was so tired and lethargic.
- My brain didn't work properly, and it was hard to concentrate.
- I couldn't stop thinking about it.
- There was a nagging feeling of emptiness.
- I had physical symptoms such as irritability, dizziness and nausea.

Then I went to my transcribed notes from women that I interviewed for this book. This is what they said:

- I felt tired all the time and would get sick with infections.
- I needed a "brain restart" because it wasn't working properly.
- I couldn't shake the feeling that something was wrong.
- I felt empty inside.
- I had a longing for things to be different.
- I was showing physical signs of stress.

When I compared the above descriptions, I could see the overlap. We have created a society that values physical needs (rightly so) and ignores spiritual needs (not so right). It's almost as if we have developed a mindset that says, "If we can't see it, it doesn't exist." We can value and acknowledge physical hunger because there's a tangible cause, but we have greater difficulty acknowledging Soul hunger because the cause is not quite so obvious.

Recognizing that many modern-day women are experiencing some degree of Soul hunger is a wake-up call to begin listening to the longings of our Souls. When the outer expression of a woman's life honors her Soul--she thrives in her health relationships and the contribution she makes in the world. When she doesn't, Soul hunger often shows up as health problems, anxiety, depression, relationship troubles, lack of fulfillment and a sense that something is missing. Our Souls thrive on space, creativity, self-expression, freedom, connection, expansion, growth, love, nature, presence, forgiveness, and self-compassion. Soul hunger is a symptom that in some way we're not feeding the Soul what it needs. Awakening to this realization is what the inner journey is all about.

The Process of Awakening

Awakening is about beginning to see things in our lives clearly and often differently. We are diminishing the role our Small Self plays in our lives, thereby creating space for our Soul to flourish. Our Soul that is often eclipsed by our Small Self is becoming brighter and acting as a powerful force and light within us. It's as if we are waking up from a long sleep where our entire life was viewed through the lens of our conditioned ways of thinking, being, feeling, and seeing the world. Because you decided to read this book, there's a good chance you're being called to awaken and bring your life back into alignment with the needs of your Soul. You're being asked to view your life with a new set of glasses that give you clarity and expanded vision so that your Soul can evolve.

Awakening is about realizing that we are spiritual beings having a human experience. We begin to recognize that we are not only physical beings, but that we are energetic beings connected with an intelligent universe. This understanding causes us to be different in our lives as we begin to see how we're all connected—and that the idea we're all separate from each other is really an illusion.

As we cultivate the qualities that align with our Souls rather than our Smaller Self, we increase our capacity for compassion, love, forgiveness, inner peace, and gratitude.

Awakening also creates an opportunity for us to bring our lives into alignment with the needs of our Soul. Each of us is born with a Soul that contains a blueprint about who we're meant to become. The Soul that accompanies our physical body into this world has a specific agenda of sorts and has accumulated experiences from previous lifetimes. It's why the term "old Soul" resonates with so many of us. We intuitively know that people don't come into this world as blank slates. If you've had children, you know what I mean. Each one is unique and has come through us so that they have an opportunity to experience certain things that their Souls require to grow and evolve. Our Soul evolves over many lifetimes and we all come in to this life at different places in the evolution of our consciousness. Each of our lifetimes give us what we need and not what we want in order to serve the evolutionary needs of our Soul.

Our Small Self, which is fuelled by fear and resistance to change, will go to great lengths to prevent us from connecting with and expressing our Souls. We must shed the limits of our Small Self so that we may be guided by our Soul. This includes the shedding of misbeliefs, conditioning, and past experiences that keep us stuck and feeling as if we're not fully thriving in our lives.

We are all on a journey towards wholeness, whereby the outer expressions of our lives are completely aligned with our Soul's agenda and spiritual laws. The greater the gap between our Soul's needs and how we live our lives, the more we experience *Soul hunger*. This suffering manifests uniquely in each of us, taking the form of emotional and/or physical issues. The key to evolving from our Small Self to a Soul or spirit-inspired life is awareness. Our consciousness and Soul both evolve through becoming increasingly aware in our lives.

All of us, either in this lifetime or subsequent ones, will reach a time where we feel so divided, that we have no choice but to cross over the suffering threshold into a new way of being. This often comes at a time when we're asking: *What is the purpose of my life? Is this all there is? Who am I? Why am I here? What is the reason for my suffering?* This threshold represents a turning point in our lives where we shift from living with no or minimal awareness to a willingness to begin to see our lives and explore what this suffering or inner restlessness is trying to teach us. Crossing this threshold is often difficult as we are being challenged to let go of the old ways of being that feel comfortable and familiar, to a new way of being that has yet to emerge. It's like a trapeze artist who knows they must let go of one bar so they can grab on to the next bar. The space in between feels risky and calls for a certain amount of faith. Some people decide to never let go, because the pull of the Small Self is stronger than the pull of the Soul to return to wholeness.

On this journey of awakening to the truth of who we are at our core, many of us get confused about how to toggle back and forth between living our lives as spiritual beings having a human experience. We are being called to nurture and care for our Small Self, which may require psychological work, while still paying attention to our Soul, which is fed by spiritual practices that involve silence, contemplation, and integration into our lives. We are effectively healing as we are closing the gap between our Small Self and our Soul.

John Welwood, a clinical psychologist who has had a large impact on bridging Western psychology with meditation and mindfulness coined the term "spiritual bypassing." In his book, *Toward a Psychology of Awakening: Buddhism, Psychotherapy and the Path of Personal and Spiritual Transformation,* Welwood describes how he had noticed that many people on a spiritual path had a "tendency to use spiritual practice to bypass or avoid dealing with certain personal or emotional 'unfinished business'" (2000, p.11). I mention this because I believe it's critical on the road to awakening that we are being called, as Welwood says, to both "grow up and wake up" (p. 231). This involves a commitment to address the ways in which our Small Self is limiting the expression of our Souls.

My journey of awakening and transformation was the perfect example of my need to "grow up and wake up." The meditation and mindfulness practices opened the door for me to "wake up." Without these tools, I wouldn't have known where I needed to grow up. I couldn't see what wasn't working. I began to see and feel what was going on inside me as well as in my outer life as expressed through my relationships, health, and vocation. I became aware of how my past conditioning and cultural beliefs were playing out in my life, causing me to behave like a victim, where I reacted in a mindless childlike fashion, rather than using my relationships as an opportunity for mature adult growth.

As we increase our awareness through meditation and mindfulness, we may find that we need to pause the "waking up" process to do some "growing up." This is when we move back and forth between the psychological work and the spiritual work. When I began the awakening journey, I didn't need psychological work as much as I needed to understand and feed my Soul. I needed tools and practices to look inside myself for answers. With increasing awareness, I was then better able to zero in on what I needed to change to be a highly functioning adult. I would spend the majority of my energy on the work of "waking up" with infrequent visits to a counsellor to get a psychological tune—up in order to "grow up." Others may need more psychological work to sort through how they have been impacted by trauma or deep wounds as a child. In these situations, "growing up" and moving through deep-seated issues requires more psychological support with meditation and mindfulness sprinkled in to support the process.

For our Souls to thrive, we need to commit to the journey of both waking up and growing up. The remainder of this book primarily focuses on waking up with the understanding that all of us on the waking up journey will come face to face with ways in which we need to grow up. We are being called to thrive in our personal lives as well as our spiritual lives. Neglecting either one of these will result in Soul hunger.

When I was climbing to the top of Mount Kilimanjaro, it was my Soul that was hungry. I had reached my *suffering threshold*. My Soul was hungry to be listened to and for a transformation to occur in my life. Like many women, I had no idea about transformation or Soul hunger or what the intelligent life force had in store for me. I just knew that there was a deep inner longing for things to change. While I didn't understand it at the time, *my Soul was calling for me to shift from living a life based on how I should be and what I should do, to how I was meant to be and who I was meant to become.* The way in which this change unfolded is the next part of the journey and involves a transformation to a new way of being.

Awakening Your Soul

Misbelief: You will find what's missing in your life by being busier, doing more, and searching for answers outside yourself.
Truth: You are being called to a new way of being, not a new way of doing. This new way of being is about living your life from the inside out, not the outside in.

Misbelief: You will be happier and more fulfilled when other people and the outer circumstances of your life change.
Truth: You need to change yourself; the outer circumstance of your life will follow.

Misbelief: Your sense of self and your identity are attached to your body and your mind.

Truth: Your body houses your Soul and your Soul is a unique gift from an intelligent life force or Spirit.

Practices/Reflections

1. Select a journal for your inner journey. Pick one that inspires you and makes you smile when you pick it up to write in it.

2. Begin to reflect on how you're spending your time–does it feed your Soul or is it distracting you from your Soul?

3. Do you have any practices in your life that enable you to calm your mind, deal with your emotions in a wise way, and connect with the deepest parts of your Self? If so, what are they? If not, I'm about to share some powerful ones with you.

CHAPTER 2

Climbing Your Inner Mountain of Transformation

As I peeled away the layers that covered my Soul in darkness, I begin to see the light of who I was always meant to become, begin to shine through the openings.

—Jenna

The biggest journey of my life began when I came down off the mountain. I began the long, slow, steady journey inward to reconnect with my inner truths and what I felt was missing in my life even though I knew I had everything to be grateful for. I was deeply confused and often found myself asking: *What is wrong with me? Why can't I just be happy? Why do I feel disconnected in my marriage? What is this inner ache and restlessness telling me? Am I meant to become something more?* I was beginning to accept that this inner longing and pull wasn't going to go away and although I was terrified, I needed to do something about it.

Mark and I returned from Africa in February and by mid March I knew I needed to make some significant changes. We had been spending six months a year in Phoenix for the past couple of years, getting away from the cold winters. When we bought our place there, I knew it was very important for Mark's mental health. He really hated winters and had always dreamt of owning a place in a warm climate, to get away from the snow. After all, isn't that what everyone dreams about? Before we bought the place, we had been there a couple of times for weekend visits and when we'd returned, I said to my sister and her husband, "There's no way I'd ever buy a place in Phoenix. I really don't like it there." While I had really wanted to say "no" to this plan that Mark had for our life, I knew it was what he needed, and I had developed a mantra for our life together: *I can make it work.* So I said "yes" to his dream, knowing I'd be sacrificing myself. *Why would I go along with something I knew wouldn't be good for me? Why couldn't I say "no?" Why was I putting Mark's needs ahead of mine? Why did I feel so responsible for other people?* I tried desperately to make this "perfect" life work until finally, I realized it would never work for me.

It was a beautiful evening in Phoenix, and we were sitting outside in the backyard in front of a blazing outdoor fireplace drinking a glass of wine as the Arizona sunset lit up the sky in red, orange, and shades of purple. I turned to Mark and said, "I need to go back to Calgary. I don't exactly know why, I just know I can't stay here because I feel like I'm dying inside. I just feel really dull inside and I don't know what's wrong with me."

As Mark looked at me with confusion in his eyes, I felt sick to my stomach. At a conscious level I had no idea why I needed to be away from Phoenix and back in Calgary, I just knew that I needed to be home. I was about to embark on a journey I knew nothing about and that wouldn't be easy, but I needed to make it anyway—for the sake of my own life. Not because I was trying to save myself from some terminal illness or disease; the life I needed to save, was of a different nature. If I didn't do something and make some changes, I would slowly continue to die inside. As terrified as I was at the thought of all this, I didn't feel I had a choice.

A few days later, I was standing in the airport in Phoenix, returning home to Calgary with my parents and my dog, Molly. I didn't fully understand the forces that were at play at that time, but my parents, who were also spending winters in Phoenix, unexpectedly had to travel home to deal with a recent cancer diagnosis my dad had received. I was going home to find my Self and at the same time, I ended up being there for my parents, who were embarking on a journey of their own.

I knew this decision was a turning point in my life. I had no idea what it was a turning point for or what direction my life was going to take from there, I just knew that things would never be the same again.

The Shift from Outer to Inner

In the early 1970s, Trina Paulus wrote the book *Hope for Flowers*. It was categorized as a children's book and was a fable about life, meaning, and hope. The story was about two caterpillars named Stripe and Yellow. Stripe begins his journey when he hatches from his egg and as caterpillars do, he eats the leaf he was hatched onto. He soon begins to sense that there must be more to life than eating and he decides to go in search of what that is. He comes across a pillar that is made up of caterpillars that were all trying to get to the top. Here he meets Yellow, the female caterpillar who is also trying to get to the top.

This journey of trying to get to the top didn't feel right, so Stripe and Yellow decide to go back down and continue to spend their days together eating. Then one day Stripe's unrest and curiosity lead him back to climbing the pillar and he decides he must get to the top to see what's up there. So he says goodbye to Yellow and begins his journey to the top. As Stripe is climbing to the top, Yellow continues to eat until one day she follows her instincts, stops eating, and spins a cocoon around her.

When Yellow emerges from the cocoon, she is a butterfly and able to fly. As Yellow is transforming into a butterfly, Stripe reaches the top and wonders, "Is this all there is?" He has not reached the sky and his only view is other caterpillars trying to get to the top. Disillusioned, Stripe returns to the ground. He reunites with Yellow, who is now a butterfly, and she shows him the cocoon. He decides to make one of his own.

He goes through his own transformation, and in the end they fly off as butterflies together. *Hope for Flowers* was a powerful little story that is eerily familiar to my own journey. When I felt the pull to return home to Calgary, I was responding to the call of nature to turn inward to examine my life—and ultimately strip away those things that were holding me back from feeling fully alive. Like Stripe, I asked myself, "Is this all there is?" and instinct told me that there was more to life than how I was living. I had gotten to what most people consider to be the "top" and was confused by this feeling of emptiness and lack of fulfillment.

I was about to experience this process of transformation for myself as my instinct told me that the answers were not going to be found by looking outside myself. I was embarking on a journey of transformation that was going to shift from a life guided by my Small Self, where I lived to please others, to a life inspired by my Soul. This process of transformation that humans undergo is best understood by learning what happens when a caterpillar becomes a butterfly. When we understand this process of transformation, we begin to realize that this process of profound and lasting change is part of a universal life force and our own evolution. This process unfolds in three stages: The hungry caterpillar, the cocoon, and the butterfly.

During the hungry caterpillar phase, we're stuffing ourselves full of beliefs, thoughts, and ideas about how we should be. We're living life based on conditioned programs and habits. We're relatively unaware of the impact on our relationships, jobs, and the choices that we make. Then something happens, usually causing a lot of discomfort or suffering inside, that forces us to make some changes. These circumstances propel us to spin the cocoon and go inward. While we're going inward, it feels like a lot of work because we're seeing things we've never previously encountered. This forces us to make some changes in order to let go of all the stuff we had been gorging on. Being in the cocoon is not easy. Once we've done the work, however, we're ready to come out of the cocoon. As a butterfly, we've transformed ourselves and have become who we were always meant to be. It's still not always easy for the butterfly, but she now has inner strength and wisdom.

The following diagram highlights the process of transformation and the shift in a way of being, from living our lives based on our conditioned Small Self, to the higher needs of our Soul.

The process begins at the birth of our Soul and continues through however many lifetimes are required for our Soul to evolve into the fully awakened state. During this evolutionary process, increasing awareness enables us to connect with who we are at the core of our being. As we increase awareness, we subsequently shed our Small Self, which begins to decrease our Soul hunger and pain. Shedding our Small Self is not easy, and we will experience resistance and fear because our Small Self wants to keep us safe and in our comfort zones. It's fascinating to recognize how the process of transformation among humans is very similar to that which a caterpillar goes through to become what it was meant to be—a butterfly. Let's examine this process in a bit more detail to shed some light on what we can expect when we feel like we have no choice and are being called to make some dramatic changes in our lives.

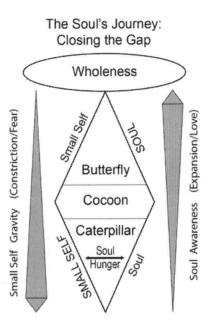

The Hungry Caterpillar

The process begins with a very hungry caterpillar hatching from an egg. The caterpillar stuffs itself with leaves, starting with the leaf onto which it emerged. As the caterpillar eats, it grows and expands at a rapid rate. During this phase, the caterpillar will shed its outgrown skin several times.

This is very similar to what women experience for the first part of our lives. At birth we all possess a Soul that is essentially whole, perfect and complete. Our Soul is here for a mission to fully express our unique way of being in the world. However, as we begin to grow and evolve, our conditioned Small Self begins to form, which slowly and gradually takes us away from our Soul. During the first seven years of our lives, we are like sponges absorbing everything with no filter to determine what our own values, needs, feelings, thoughts, wishes, desires, or unique gifts are. We are learning how to see the world and our lives through the lens of our culture, caregivers, and experiences. Whether these experiences are favorable or not isn't the point. The point is that we see the world through other people's eyes and not our own. We are "stuffing" ourselves with all sorts of beliefs and observations about who we should be, what it means to be successful, how we're meant to be in our relationships, what it means to be a "good" woman, wife, mother, and friend, and what we should value. In short, we are stuffing ourselves with all sorts of misbeliefs that impact every choice, thought, and action—and ultimately how our life unfolds.

We are growing at a rapid rate, but for most of us, we're growing further away from our true nature and who we're meant to become. We are learning how we are *supposed* to be rather than who we are *meant* to be. It's during this "stuffing" phase of our development that we accumulate the stories. Stories about how we've been hurt, betrayed, belittled, and/or judged; or conversely, how we've been loved, respected, supported, and nourished. These stories are what form the fabric of our lives and the shedding that we are often trying to do, is shedding the stories about ourselves that keep us stuck.

In addition to accumulating the stories, we're accumulating a lot of other peoples' opinions in our heads. We get to a point in our development that we have gorged so much, accumulated so many stories and opinions, that we feel heavy and weighed down. We're so full of other peoples' stuff, that we have no room for our Soul. Complicating this scenario is that fact that most of us are not aware about how this conditioning and gorging is playing out in our lives. We blame the outer circumstances of our lives, rather than understanding that the inner conditioning and our Small Self is manifesting in the outer aspects of our lives.

This is how it felt for me on the way up Mount Kilimanjaro. I carried a whole lot of stuff that weighed me down. I carried the beliefs about what it meant to be a "good" woman and what my role was meant to be in the world. I carried the belief that my success and value as a human being was based on how smart I was, how many degrees I had, and how much I sacrificed myself for other people. I was used to listening to my Small Self, which told me I was meant to be quiet and respectful and not rock the boat. Because my Small Self needed to be accepted, liked, and approved of, I was accumulating anger and resentment as I compromised my Soul. I was also weighed down by feelings that had become stuck in my body, because I didn't give myself the permission to feel them. In short, this accumulation of stuff that resulted from living from my Small Self left no room for my Soul.

We often don't realize or fully appreciate how this extra weight and living in a way that doesn't align with the truth about who we are, starves our Soul. We have accumulated a lot of garbage, and most women don't know how to close the gap between who we are and who we're meant to be. Just like the caterpillar that needs to shed its skin, we need to learn how to shed our stories and limiting beliefs about ourselves so that we can decrease our Soul hunger and begin to thrive again.

Many women get stuck at this phase of feeling full of old stories and other peoples' opinions and don't know how to do the shedding. The sad truth is that being stuck in this phase and not going through the shedding and transformation will impact our emotional, physical, and spiritual health. I think this is why so many women are depressed, anxious, sick, and in bad relationships. We can't thrive because we're not meant to go through life carrying around all this stuff. And most importantly, we're not meant to mold our lives around what we feel we "should" be.

The Cocoon

The need to "cocoon" is a normal and natural part of the process of transformation. Once the caterpillar has gorged and grown enough, it stops eating, hangs upside down, and spins itself a silky cocoon. Within the protective casing, the caterpillar radically transforms by digesting itself as it releases enzymes to dissolve all its tissues. Certain cells survive the digestive process and then are used to form the features of the adult butterfly.

It is during this phase that the dramatic transformation occurs. During the previous phase, the caterpillar did a lot of shedding, but in the end it was still a caterpillar. In this phase, however, all the work being done inside the cocoon results in transforming the caterpillar into a butterfly and into an entirely new way of being in the world—with an entirely different purpose. To do this shedding, we need to develop a keen and intense awareness about what is going on inside us. We need to shift our attention from outward to inward so that we begin to see our lives more clearly.

When I arrived back in Calgary, leaving Mark in Phoenix, I went into a cocoon. It was a very painful time in my life. It was as if the suffering had reached a threshold and forced me into the cocoon, but I intuitively knew the inner discomfort would become greater if I didn't begin the inner journey. This was the beginning of my radical shift into a new way of being.

In the past, I had always been a very social person and any spare time I had, I arranged to get together with friends. For most of my life, I felt uncomfortable being by myself, so I found myself confused by this need to spend time alone. Other than going to the odd appointment with my dad, who was dealing with cancer, I had a lot of time on my hands. My family and friends wondered what was going on and why I had left Mark behind in Phoenix. Was our marriage in trouble? The hardest part was that I had no answer because I really had no idea.

I didn't know where to begin to figure out what needed to change in my life. I turned to my old standby when I'm feeling confused— my books. Part of the problem was that I didn't know what kind of books to look for. As I settled in with a cup of tea a few days after arriving home, I went to the bookcase in my bedroom to see if there was a book that sparked my interest. At that point, words like transformation, spirituality, consciousness, awakening, or the Soul weren't in my vocabulary. The only things in my awareness were a feeling of being dull inside and an ache for something more.

As I read over all the titles, a book jumped out at me: *Discover Your Destiny: The 7 Stages of Self-Awakening* by Robin Sharma. I didn't recall buying the book; perhaps there had been something stirring in me for a while that I wasn't aware of or able to put my finger on. I grabbed the book and my tea, snuggled into my bed, and cracked open the book. I read many things in that volume that stirred something in me. In retrospect, I know that it was speaking to my Soul. There was one quote in particular that jumped out at me: "I am not on this earth by chance. I am here for a purpose and that purpose is to grow into a mountain, not to shrink to a grain of sand" (2004, p. 83). That was it—I had always believed, if not consciously, then at least subconsciously, that I was here for a purpose, and I had given that up when I decided to retire and live a life of leisure. I may have climbed a real mountain, but I was not growing and could relate to the idea of shrinking.

My life had become stagnant, and if there's one thing the Soul can't and won't tolerate, is being stifled and small. In the front of my journal that I was keeping during this time, I jotted down a number of quotes by Joseph Campbell as cited by Diane Osbon in *Reflections on the Art of Living: A Joseph Campbell Companion*. These quotes foreshadowed what was about to come in relation to my journey. They spoke to me and may speak to you if there is something in you stirring to awaken:

> "The heroic life is living the individual adventure. There is no security in following the call to adventure. Nothing is exciting if you know what the outcome is going to be. To refuse the call means stagnation. What you don't experience positively you will experience negatively. You enter the forest at the darkest point, where there is no path. Where there is a way or path, it is someone else's path. You are not on your own path. If you follow someone else's way, you are not going to realize your potential" (1991, p. 21-24).

I had been refusing the call and my Soul was saying *no more*. I was starting to get a sense that I had been following someone else's path and was now about to embark on my own. It was becoming apparent to me that my path could only be found within my Self. How this would all unfold was unclear, and from Joseph Campbell's wisdom, I began to get the idea this was exactly how it was meant to be.

The cocoon phase is about turning the spotlight on our own life for a while in order to become aware. We stop paying so much attention to what others are doing and not doing. We are drawn to go on our own inner journey. With the spotlight on ourselves, we can begin to see that the things we've been gorging on are holding us back and keeping us small. We also begin to see the misbeliefs that are holding us back, keeping us fearful, or preventing us from growing and becoming who we're meant to be. The transformation happens when we radically strip away all those things and establish a new way of being. We shift from being guided by our Small

Self, which leaves us living in fear, to being guided by our Soul, which is led by an intelligent universe and the energy of love.

You may be wondering, "Isn't it selfish to be so focused on yourself?" I had many people question what I was doing and wondered how I could leave Mark all alone in Phoenix. Didn't I realize how lucky I was? It was a difficult time for me as I sensed I was being judged—often harshly—for what I was doing. One of my biggest fears was being viewed as "self-centered," so turning all my attention inward was uncomfortable after having always been so outwardly focused on everyone else. When you think back to the butterfly, you realize there comes a time when the caterpillar needs to spin the cocoon so the transformation can occur. The caterpillar doesn't stay in the cocoon forever; it resurfaces in a way that contributes greater beauty to the world. It's a necessary part of the process—just as the inner journey is a necessary part of the process you need to go through in order to shed and transform whatever is holding you back from becoming a butterfly.

During this part of the transformation, you need space and time to focus on your Self and your life. The caterpillar goes into the cocoon by itself and hangs upside down. It's not hanging upside down with its husband, boyfriend, family members, or anyone else. It is hanging upside down, by itself. This alone time doesn't mean we're depressed or dysfunctional, or that it's going to last forever. When women are going through this they often have no idea why they need to be by themselves; they just do. This is often a very confusing time, especially when we are turning our attention away from others.

When I share this part of my journey where I needed to be by myself in my own cocoon as part of the process to shed what wasn't serving my highest good and connect with my Soul, I had many women ask, "What if I don't have the luxury of being away and doing that inner work? How do I do that while in the middle of my busy life?" The truth is that undergoing a transformation and establishing a new way of being requires energy and space. It's all part of the process and if we don't give ourselves the space, we may be forced to create it when the symptoms of Soul hunger get worse and impact our physical or emotional health.

I had lunch with my friend Jenna the other day, and she told me how she needed to "cocoon" for a short period of time in the midst of a busy life so that she could create space to connect with her Soul. Jenna had recently left her job as an executive assistant to take on a new challenge managing a department. She described how she had been in the new job for several months and was finding it stressful. She had a hard time coping with the extra demands of this position and found herself feeling emotional. She had even broken down at work and begun crying, which was unlike her. She had always prided herself in her work and had very high expectations about her performance.

As we sat through lunch together, she described how she knew this was signaling her to do some inner Soul searching to determine where the source of this stress was coming from. She shared how she was pulling back from social commitments she normally loved and instead was spending time at home, snuggled on her couch with her dog, doing some reading and reflecting. She just didn't have the energy, nor did she feel like being out and about when she needed to get to the "root" of what was causing her to feel this way.

She described how, in the past, her choice might have been to quit the job, but as she got to know herself better, she realized running from the job wasn't the answer. The answer was to create space in her life, go into her "cocoon" for a while, and connect with herself to understand what her Soul was telling her and what she was meant to learn. She realized the answer might be that this wasn't the job that feeds her Soul and that she would need to make some decisions. But she was willing to stick with the discomfort, uncover some beliefs that led her to feel she needed to be perfect and in control all the time, and stick with the often uncomfortable process of inner growth.

My role as a compassionate mentor is to ensure the transformation isn't botched and to light the way for what is often a confusing time for women. I've undergone the transformation in my own life, and I know how scary it can be. Because I've been there and navigated the process in my own life, I have tools to help women let go of their Small Self so they can fully embrace their Essential Self based on the needs of their Souls.

I stayed in my own cocoon for several months. During this time, I was introduced to meditation, mindfulness, and other spiritual practices. I began to learn that while these practices are becoming increasingly popular, it's not really about the practices. It's about the ability to look inside ourselves for answers and manage our minds. The practices help us improve our health, which is often impacted by years of carrying garbage around. We learn how to be more compassionate with ourselves and how to love ourselves unconditionally. We become skilled at dealing with all our feelings and learn how to honor what we need. We transform the toxicity of anger and resentment into fuel for inspired action. We become proficient at connecting with an intelligent life force that opens our channels for intuition and creativity, which helps our Soul to emerge.

The Butterfly Emerges

When the caterpillar's process of transformation is complete, the butterfly will emerge and move through the world in a new way. It has shed its previous form and transformed itself into its fullest expression of itself.

I would have to say that when I came out of the cocoon the most radical part of my transformation was complete. That's not to say I didn't have work left to do or that I was done growing, as that will continue for the rest of my life, but I did come out with a new way of being that created a ripple of changes. I began thriving again.

I came out of retirement and founded a business so that I could mentor other women who are being called to undergo a transformation. For the first time in my life, I noticed I liked being by myself and cherished the space to engage in my spiritual practices. I made decisions that aligned with my Soul and made an agreement with myself that I wouldn't compromise my Soul for anyone or any situation. I began to honor my intuition and inner knowing instead of being stuck in my head all the time trying to "figure it out." I became kinder, gentler, and more loving and accepting of my imperfections and myself. I learned to be in tune with both my Small Self and my Soul and made the choice to place my Soul in the driver's seat. I developed a deep and meaningful connection with the divine life force in the universe.

While I have created a new way of being, I must confess that I still binge eat while watching Netflix, drink too much diet Coke, fall out of an exercise routine, get irritated when people push my buttons, get stuck in my head at times, forget to floss my teeth, am judgmental, check Facebook too much, and occasionally indulge in one too many glasses of wine. My new mantra is that "I'm going for progress not perfection."

My relationship with Mark also underwent a transformation, which began when I came out of the cocoon. Our connection became deeper and more spiritual. We realized we were together so each of us could grow as spiritual beings, and not just for survival, having children, and meeting each other's Small Self needs.

Whether a relationship will survive when only one person goes through a transformation is unclear. In our case, we became like Stripe and Yellow where we both began to examine our lives. I was forced by my Soul to undergo a transformation, and I think Mark would agree that he was forced by my transformation to begin looking at his own life.

The transformation of our marriage in many ways mirrored the individual transformation I went through. The pre-transformation years of our marriage were based on the need to complete each other. We both brought our own "garbage" that we had accumulated. That's why these close relationships provide a big catalyst for change. They push absolutely every button there is in us and create so much discomfort in our lives that we shut down all together and either become roommates, get separated, or do the work necessary to come out the other side with a relationship based on our Soul's need to grow, rather than the Small Self's need for survival. When we are in relationships with people who either have or are willing to do the work to transform from a caterpillar to a butterfly, our Souls thrive.

As I came out of my cocoon, I realized that not only did I use certain practices to facilitate my transformation, but I also used them in very specific ways. I didn't use them for spiritual entertainment, but rather to create a container for lasting transformation and change.

Spiritual Entertainment or Transformation

Women entertain themselves with all sorts of things including drumming circles, crystals, angel cards, energy balancing, chakra cleansing, new moon meditations, singing bowls, prayer groups and countless other things. I call it entertainment because we often use these activities to keep us busy and yet they don't change our lives in any significant way. They become one more thing to keep us distracted. It's ironic that these practices that are intended to help us connect with ourselves can actually serve to distract us from what is going on in our lives that keeps us disconnected from our Souls.

There is an important difference between using these tools as entertainment and using them for transformation. With the increasing interest in spirituality and spiritual practices, I believe it's a difference we need to be aware of. I don't think there's anything wrong with using these practices for spiritual entertainment as long as they fit with our intention. For example, I have many women coming to me who have been on a spiritual path for a long time. They may have read a lot of books, attended numerous workshops, and joined different meditation groups without having found what they are searching for. This is because meditation and mindfulness can also be used as spiritual entertainment without resulting in lasting and significant changes. Expanding our toolkits in service of our Soul is different than using these practices to keep us distracted from our growth and evolution.

This idea is explored in the book, *Living Deeply: The Art & Science of Transformation in Everyday Life*. Marilyn Mandala Schlitz, Cassandra Vieten, and Tina Amorok highlighted the findings from the Institute of Noetic Sciences' decade-long study into transformation. The study found that a transformation of consciousness comes from "profound internal shifts that result in long-lasting changes in the way you experience and relate to yourself, others, and the world" (2007, pp. 14-15). It goes on to explain that this shift doesn't make you a different person, rather it helps you connect with who you are at your core "independent of the social expectations and cultural conditioning that had previously shaped" your sense of Self (p. 15). Imagine knowing who you are and being able to shed all the beliefs and thoughts about yourself that are holding you back from stepping fully into your most authentic and amazing Self.

The authors identified four essential elements for a practice to result in a transformation. When the practices that you're integrating into your life contain these four elements, you are most definitely primed for transformation. These elements are **intention, attention, repetition, and guidance**. The transformation I'm talking about in this book, and that I underwent in my own life, was a process that included these four elements.

When we use meditation and mindfulness for transformation, we're using the practices to find answers within ourselves. We will never awaken or connect with our Souls when we don't have the tools to do so. Meditation and mindfulness are the only practices I'm aware of that help you look deeply within yourself so you can get to know your Self. They also help you connect with your intuition so you can be guided by your Essential Self.

The practice of mindfulness, which is all about awareness, helps us to see things and feel things we hadn't previously seen or allowed ourselves to feel. Without the ability to develop this attention and awareness, our lives are primarily about living out pre-programmed conditioning in a mindless fashion. As Socrates pointed out, "the unexamined life is not worth living." We must examine our life to change it—and to feel fully alive.

The need for repetition is essential for us to experience the transformation we may not want but know we need. Growing into this new way of being involves creating new habits. In the same way that one day of strength training won't transform our muscle mass, one day of meditation won't result in transformation. Instead, once we begin our short daily spiritual practices, we begin to feel shifts. We begin to feel differently inside and more empowered. It doesn't take long before we *need* our daily practices to feel our best. When we get to this stage, the practices become an integral part of our life, much like brushing our teeth.

Having guidance is critical for transformation. Anyone can lead a meditation and provide a nice experience in the moment, but not anyone can lead a transformation. Transformation is about integrating what we're learning into our real life and being different. *It's not about doing more; it's about being different.* This is one area where many women fall short. Instruction is essential for creating a transformative practice.

In addition to knowing how to do the actual practices correctly, the process of transformation is often hard. Without a mentor we often get stuck, and it takes women longer if they're trying to figure it out on their own. Without the tools and the right kind of support, it can feel almost hopeless—as if you're trying to build a house and you don't have the tools or the necessary materials. One of my clients put it this way: "The process of change and transformation was really hard. The change was hard because I was seeing things for the first time and I was literally having to go through a period of purging, which was really hard." It is particularly hard for those of us who have never tuned into ourselves and have spent most of our lives tuning out or focused on other people.

We will now begin to explore the practices and wisdom that will aid you on your awakening journey. As I came to understand in my own life, the journey needs to begin with learning how to settle our busy minds in order to give our bodies a deep state of rest. We need to develop the ability to feel strong and resilient in our lives; not only when things are going well, but more importantly when we're in the midst of chaos. Like many people being called to awaken the deepest parts of their Selves, I was about to come face to face with an ancient practice that I was deeply resistant to—meditation.

Awakening Your Soul

Misbelief: The inner call for transformation with the accompanying yearning, restlessness, and desire to be different—or the feeling that something is missing—will go away on its own.
Truth: When you are called to awaken there is nothing wrong with you. The inner pull and urges will not go away until you answer the call. Ignoring the call will impact your physical, emotional, and spiritual health.

Misbelief: You can radically transform your life with minimal commitment to dabbling in spiritual practices or self-care.
Truth: Transformation to a new way of being requires space and a willingness to look deeply inside your Self. Research has shown that a new way of being arises from your intentions, level of awareness, willingness to commit to practices, and a guide to support you.

Misbelief: You'll be "living the life" and completely fulfilled when you have material abundance, security, and a stable relationship, and when those closest to you are happy and settled.
Truth: The shift from living your life based on the needs of the Small Self to your Soul often involves an inner crisis, as old ways of being fall away to create space for what has yet to emerge. This is often a confusing and unsettling time.

Practices/Reflections

1. If your Soul could speak, what would it say to you about your relationships, your health and your connection with an intelligent life force?

2. Are you able and willing to create space in your life for transformation? What would your life look like if you slowed it down?

3. What are your intentions for any spiritual practices that you have or plan to introduce into your life?

CHAPTER 3

It's Not About Surviving— It's About Thriving

As my mind became calmer and more settled, my life became clearer. I began to know what I needed in order to be happy and I felt a sense of contentment that I had never experienced before.
— Olivia

My first experience with meditation was on a day that became the turning point in my life. It was the start of a long journey home to my Self. It was the beginning—but of what? I really had no idea. It felt like I was in a Star Trek movie with battles to fight and unknown adventures to take. There were other forces at play and I didn't understand that they were urging me to create a new way of being.

As I was finally sitting down to meditate for the very first time, after battling resistance for most of the morning, the phone rang. It was my mom. After giving me the scoop about my dad's cancer treatments and her grocery list of doctor's appointments, she asked how I was doing being back in Calgary without Mark. Before I had a chance to answer, she said, "I'm really concerned about your marriage. This separation is not good for you. I was telling your dad that couples your age should be having sex more often, and that is not going to happen when you're spending all this time apart. It's really not normal." I was speechless and could feel myself going red. When I finally opened my mouth, I managed a fake laugh and said, "Mom, don't worry about it. Mark and I are going to be just fine." While the words were coming out of my mouth, I wondered why I didn't say what was really on my mind: *Maybe it's more appropriate that you focus on your own marriage and I'll focus on mine. And what I really need is support right now instead of further judgment.*

As I hung up the phone I thought, *Now I'm too agitated to meditate.* The conversation with my mom had really stirred up stuff in me. But I told myself, *What the hell, Bev; it's only five minutes. Just sit down and do it.* Overcoming what felt like a mountain of resistance, I finally sat down to close my eyes and tune in to my Self. I had decided to give meditation a try by starting with five minutes a day. As soon as my eyes closed I was immediately aware of my scattered mind. *This is what a monkey mind feels like,* I thought. It was all over the place. From the conversation with my mom, to my grocery list, to wondering *What the hell am I doing back in Calgary when I could be floating around in the pool in Phoenix with Mark.* It stirred up the inner knowing that the conversation with my mom was yet another example of not using my voice. And maybe she was right and my marriage *was* in trouble.

My road to meditation began just before Mark and I left to climb Mount Kilimanjaro. I went to see an integrative medicine doctor because my body was starting to show the signs of this inner turmoil. It was around the same time that I also saw the therapist, trying to figure out what was going on with me. My body and my mind both seemed to be letting me down. I had gained a lot of weight, which stuck like glue no matter what I did; I wasn't sleeping very well; my mind wasn't really sharp; and I was feeling stressed and empty inside, even though I kept saying to myself, *I'm retired, what have I got to be stressed about?* I assumed it had something to do with my hormones, but I had no idea how to get myself back in balance.

After I filled out countless forms and assessments and subjected myself to blood, urine, and saliva tests, the doctor told me my stress hormone, cortisol, was out of balance, which was creating a cascade of other hormonal imbalances in my body and resulting in my symptoms. This explained why a few days into our hike up the mountain, I began bleeding again. I was mortified. I hadn't had a period for a few years and wasn't prepared for this little surprise. Trying to pin toilet paper to my underwear and deal with that on top of peeing along the trail ten times a day (as a result of the diuretic to combat elevation sickness), was a challenge. I began to wonder, *Could the emotional turmoil and confusion that I was feeling be causing the cortisol imbalance and these physical problems?* It was my first direct experience with the idea that not living our truths, using our voices, feeling disconnected in relationships and trying to make things work when they weren't could have a physical impact on our health. How many other physical and emotional issues experienced by women are caused by what I call Soul hunger and pain? I think lots!

I came to learn that hormones are like a symphony, and if one is out of whack they all are. My cortisol imbalance was resulting in every other hormone being out of balance. No wonder I wasn't sleeping, found myself gaining weight, had a racing mind and generally felt like crap. I also knew that while these things were just annoying at this point, if left unchecked, they could turn into more significant health issues.

As my doctor finished educating me about hormones, she looked at my history and noticed that I hadn't checked off meditation on the form. She asked, "Have you ever thought about learning to meditate?" I sheepishly responded, "No, I actually haven't, but I suppose I can give it a try." It felt a little deceitful because to be honest, she caught me off guard with the meditation thing and I had no intention of giving it a try. I thought, *There is no way I can sit there and do nothing. How can that really make that much of a difference? What a waste of time!* I left her office that day thinking, *I'm sure there are other things I can do instead.*

I put the whole meditation thing on a shelf, went to Africa and then returned—still with no intention of giving it a try. The closest I came was downloading an audiobook about it, which I quickly passed over because it all seemed a little too "out there" and complicated for me.

Then, shortly after returning to Calgary and going into my cocoon, I heard about a talk at our local health store on how to use diet to improve your stress levels. I thought, *That's perfect; I'll spend a couple of hours learning about that and then take some steps to improve my stress levels. I'm sure I'll learn about supplements and other tips and I'll be good to go.*

I arrived a few minutes early and settled in to hear the speaker, who was an expert on nutrition and health. I was hopeful about getting some tips, so I was tuned in to everything he said. But before he said even one word about nutrition, he paused and said, "If you want to detoxify your body, you need to detoxify your mind."

He went on to say everyone should have a meditation practice of some sort and couldn't stop talking about how important it was to detoxify your mind if you want to be healthy. His message caught me off guard, but I noticed my resistance to the idea of meditation was beginning to soften. His comments, combined with what my previous doctor had said, sparked a curiosity in me. *Maybe this meditation thing could help me feel calmer inside and help with some of the issues I was having.* I was about to learn that settling my mind would lead me closer to my Soul and ultimately to finding and using my voice.

Once I began practicing meditation, I soon noticed that I looked forward to my few minutes a day where I would tune out the world to tune into my Self. I began to feel calmer inside, even though I couldn't explain why. I also noticed that as the trial month I had signed up for was coming to an end, I began to wonder, *What am I going to do when it ends? Do I keep listening to the same thing over and over? What is this really all about? Am I doing it correctly?* The nurse in me had a big need to understand why and how this meditation thing worked, and so I went back online to find a class or course I could take to learn more about it. I came across an afternoon workshop at the local Buddhist Centre for beginning meditators and thought, *This is perfect, I'm going to drag one of my friends along and learn how to meditate.*

We arrived at the Centre on a beautiful sunny spring day and climbed the stairs to the second level. It honestly felt more like an office building than a spot where meditators and spiritual people would hang out. As we walked inside, I noticed it was decked out in all kinds of Buddhist paraphernalia, but since I was not Buddhist, I had no idea what any of it really meant. We settled into our chairs and then a woman with a shaved head and robe came in and sat at the front of the room. She talked a little about meditation and some Buddhist teachings and then lead us in a couple of practices. To be honest, I don't recall what the practices were and although it was a lovely afternoon, I went away as confused about meditation as I had been when I arrived. I felt peaceful and calm, but I still had no idea *how* to do "it" and what "it" actually was.

Now I was really curious. I went on the hunt to learn more about this mysterious yet powerful thing. All I had as an image of meditation were people sitting around cross-legged on the floor with their eyes closed, holding their hands in some funny position. I really had no idea what people were actually doing with their eyes closed. I was also a little concerned because I had heard about people going on multi-day silent meditation retreats where they sat on the floor for hours on end and I thought, *There's no way I can do that.*

Back online, I searched for "meditation training" and came across a site that jumped out at me. It was the McLean Meditation Institute® in Sedona, Arizona, founded by Sarah McLean who wrote the book *Soul-Centered: Transform Your Life in 8 Weeks with Meditation.* Sarah offered meditation workshops and teacher training for people who were interested in meditation from a "secular" perspective. She had spent many years in monasteries and ashrams and was a long-time meditator who created the SEED Meditation Method. SEED stands for the "Simple, Easy, Every Day™" meditation method. That sounded perfect for me! I wanted something that didn't involve religious or spiritual practices and that was simple and easy to do.

For the next eight months I studied and practiced meditation and eventually became certified as a meditation and mindfulness teacher. I read books, experimented with various techniques, and ultimately learned how to quiet my mind, work with my feelings, develop my intuition, and connect with my Soul. I was transforming my way of being and getting to know my Self for the very first time. It was during those months that I learned how to look inside myself for answers to allow that inner knowing and the voice of my Soul to guide my life.

A few months after I started my daily meditation practice, I returned to my doctor and she reported that my stress hormone cortisol was back in balance. The only thing I had done differently was meditate. Many of my symptoms began to go away and I was starting to feel like I was thriving again. It wasn't like I was my old self, it was like my true Self had been revealed to me. At last I began to understand what all the stress was about in my life that played such havoc on my cortisol and my ability to fit into my clothes.

The Soul Sapping Effects of Inner Stress

Like many women, I spent many years of my life juggling all sorts of demands from taking my kids to soccer and hockey practices, to doing the laundry, grocery shopping and holding down a job. While Mark put all his energy into making money and climbing the corporate ladder, I took on the lion's share of the emotional load of raising the kids, running our home life, and organizing childcare so I could pursue my passion for nursing on a part-time basis. My main priority for many years was trying to maintain the delicate balance between what my Soul needed and what my roles needed, and I would often feel frazzled. Most nights I found myself tossing and turning as my mind went over the previous day or thought about what I had to get done the next day.

While my weekdays were consumed with shuffling the demands of work, kids, and household responsibilities, weekends were the time for me to have some fun. Mark and I would get the occasional babysitter so that we could go out and socialize with friends or unwind. But by the end of the weekend, instead of feeling rested and rejuvenated, I'd feel exhausted and pour myself into bed Sunday night, ready to start all over again on Monday morning.

Despite being a relatively healthy, fit, and happy woman, I found myself experiencing frequent tension headaches and the occasional migraine. I knew I spent a lot of time in my head and was a bit of a worrywart. I also thought all of this was "normal" and knew that although I often felt stressed, I was at a loss as to how to handle that stress. I frequently felt an inner tension and as hard as I tried to contain it, I had moments where I snapped like a rubber band.

I remember one summer day when my kids were home and seemed to be doing everything possible to get under my skin. I lost it and began screaming at them. I sounded like a raging lunatic. A few days later, my niece, laughing, said that her friend happened to be living in the house behind me and commented, "Wow, your Aunt Bev is a total bitch. You should have heard her yelling at her kids." Definitely not one of my finer moments!

I knew I needed to learn to be more patient, but I really didn't know how to develop that skill. I didn't know how to release the stress in the moment and, as a result, I had headaches for years. Other than taking ibuprofen, which I called my "vitamin I," I had very few tools in my toolkit to help me get to the root cause.

When my children grew up and left home, I experienced a different kind of stress. It wasn't the stress of perpetual motion, it was the stress of *"who am I now that my role as a mom has changed?"* This confusion and uncertainty about my very sense of identity was amplified when I retired. The stress that had accumulated from a busy life raising a family was now compounded by the stress of a Soul that was hungry and feeling stagnant. It was like layers upon layers of stress had accumulated even while in many ways, I was living a beautiful and fulfilling life.

Despite having been a nurse for many years, I didn't fully appreciate the significance of stress in my own life or the way it manifests. Emotional stress plays an important role in most women's lives and it's often insidious. Being stressed feels normal for us, but we need to realize it's *not* normal and it's a sign we need to make some changes.

In addition to being in the perpetual state of motion needed for getting things done, many of us have the belief that *when things outside of us are settled, then we can feel settled.* We believe that when we have the right job, no family conflict, the kids are happy, the next vacation is planned, we're getting along with our partners, and we have enough money, that we won't feel stressed. This is in fact one of the biggest barriers to achieving what we all desire, which is inner contentment and peace.

If there is one thing that disconnects us from our Soul, it is stress. Especially the Soul-sapping chronic stress, which goes on for extended periods of time and wears us down physically, emotionally, and spiritually. It doesn't go away because the underlying situation is not temporary. This stress is related to Soul-sapping jobs, unhappy relationships, and/or living from our small sense of Self for too long. Stress and the Soul cannot co-exist. When we're in survival mode, we have shut down and aren't able to hear or receive messages from our Soul.

Recognizing that at any stage we can shift our body out of this perpetual state of stress through practices such as meditation, is one of the most powerful things we can do on the road to reclaiming our lives. It's about understanding we have the inner power to remain grounded and strong when life inevitably throws us a curve ball. Or knowing when we are confused about the direction we are meant to take in our lives related to a job, a relationship, or really anything, that we have the tools to tune into our Selves and find the answers.

There's no doubt that tuning in can be scary because as I have heard countless women say, "I'm afraid of what I'm going to find. What if I don't like what I see? What if what I see tells me that I need to make some changes? That's all really terrifying to me." They then ask me, "Is it worth it?" One thing I know for sure, whatever needs to change in your life to bring things back into alignment, isn't going to go away on its own. There is a powerful force in this universe and it's not going to stop trying to get your attention until you listen. Yes, it's scary. And yes, it's so worth it. There is a pot of gold waiting at the end of the rainbow.

Having a practice like meditation in your toolkit is one of the most important gifts you can give yourself. Rather than being a luxury, I have come to view it as a necessity and one that every woman needs in order to awaken her Soul.

The Truth About Meditation

Looking back, I find it entertaining and a little bit sad that my preconceived ideas about meditation became a barrier to having an open mind and giving it a try. As soon as I tried, a whole new world opened up to me. I felt I had ways and tools to not only cope but thrive in most situations that life could throw at me.

I have been studying and practicing meditation for the past few years now, and I have used these powerful practices to make some big changes in my physical and emotional health, as well as in my ability to get out of my head and tap into my intuition. These practices have shifted my very way of being from being stressed out and distracted to being more peaceful and connected with my inner wisdom.

Regardless of the increasing consensus about the benefits of meditation, it can be a bit confusing knowing where to begin. I view these meditation practices as tools to have in our toolkit that we can pull out and use, depending on what we are trying to achieve. There is a meditation practice that can help with virtually every challenge a woman may face, allowing her to get through life with greater inner peace and wisdom.

Countless practices have arisen from almost every spiritual and religious tradition, and each of them has a different perspective and way of practicing. The following diagram highlights how meditation is an umbrella term under which different practices, including mindfulness, fall:

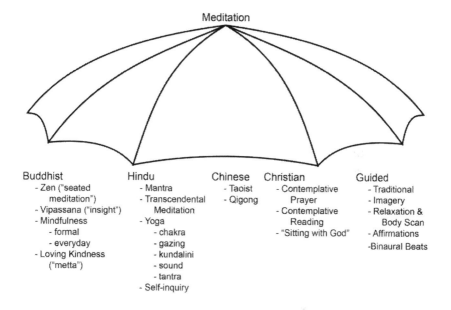

Meditation

Buddhist	Hindu	Chinese	Christian	Guided
- Zen ("seated meditation")	- Mantra	- Taoist	- Contemplative Prayer	- Traditional
- Vipassana ("insight")	- Transcendental Meditation	- Qigong	- Contemplative Reading	- Imagery
- Mindfulness	- Yoga		- "Sitting with God"	- Relaxation & Body Scan
- formal	- chakra			- Affirmations
- everyday	- gazing			-Binaural Beats
- Loving Kindness ("metta")	- kundalini			
	- sound			
	- tantra			
	- Self-inquiry			

While categorizing meditation in this way may be helpful for a broader understanding of it, I didn't find it useful from a practical and personal perspective. I needed to find a way to understand meditation that aligned with what we as women need, rather than getting caught up in continuous debates and varying opinions surrounding definitions. As women, what are we trying to achieve in our lives that can be supported by meditation and the countless available practices?

Meditation boils down to four things that we are cultivating to fully thrive in our lives. It's like we're building a cake with four tiers. Each layer of the cake is a different flavor, so it has different ingredients. We start with the bottom layer and mix the ingredients together and then pop it in the oven to get the base cake. When that layer is done, we move on to the next tier with some ingredients that are the same and a few that are different. We continue baking the cakes until we've got our four levels. Then we put the icing on the cake. When it is done, we don't see the ingredients anymore, we see only the cake.

Here are the four layers:

1. The first step in the transformation is a simple meditation practice that enables us to develop **concentration and focus.** As we learn to settle our minds and create space for silence, we give our bodies a deep state of rest. It enables us to shift out of survival mode into a restorative and nourishing way of being. Through this practice, we create an environment in our body that promotes health and healing. We cultivate the ability to be resilient from the inside out. In other words, we don't wait for all of our external circumstances to be "just so" before we thrive in our lives.

2. As our minds and bodies become settled, we develop the ability to **pay attention without judgment** to each moment. This enables us to be aware of our surroundings, thoughts, feelings, and the subtleties of our bodies, so that we gain insight and make wise choices. We develop increased awareness of our lives as they unfold, and we do this in a way that is accepting, rather than with judgment of what is arising. This is all about learning to *live in the moment* with less focus on the past and future. We learn how to be accepting, which makes us more peaceful.

3. Next, we cultivate **heart and Soul expanding qualities** such as compassion, loving kindness, gratitude, and forgiveness—both towards our Self and others. As we increase these expansive feelings and emotions, we minimize the emotions that are reflective of our small sense of Self. Emotions like anger, resentment, guilt, jealousy, sadness, and bitterness are replaced with joy, contentment, fulfillment, and gratitude. We learn the principles that enable us to attract *more* expansive emotions and ways of being.

4. Finally, we develop a **connection with an intelligent life force** that flows through us and of which we are a part of, guiding us in manifesting a fulfilling and meaningful life. This is where we cultivate intuition and inner wisdom. We get in tune with the ways in which this life force speaks to us, such as intuition, creativity, coincidences,

and synchronistic events. We use this information to guide our lives and it becomes our inner compass. As we align our outer lives with our inner knowing, we begin to thrive in our relationships, vocations, and health.

Now back to the cake. We can stop at any layer and don't need to build a higher cake, but to connect with our Souls, we really have to be all in. Our Souls are like the icing on the cake. When we connect with them and let them be the guiding light for our life, we are living and feeling fully alive.

Unfortunately, there are some commonly held misconceptions about meditation that prevent many women, including myself for many years, from benefitting from the practices that have the potential to shift our very way of being in our lives.

Meditation Misconceptions

At the beginning of every meditation workshop, I ask women: "Why do you want to learn to meditate or what brought you here?" It's not surprising that I often hear the same responses, and many times the list is surrounded in deep emotion and a desire to live more peacefully and authentically. Women share the following reasons:

- A desire to sleep better.
- Health issues caused by stress.
- Feelings of anxiety or depression.
- Wanting to not be so distracted in their relationships and lives.
- Seeking a deeper spiritual connection.
- Don't know who they are at their core.
- Have emotions they don't know how to deal with like anger and resentment.
- Would like to feel more peaceful, grounded and patient.
- Would like to set an example for their kids.
- Want to be more intuitive.

When I ask the women what is preventing them living more peacefully, better connected, and with better health, the most common response is, "I don't know how. I lack the tools."

Olivia was one of these women who wanted to feel more peaceful but didn't know where to begin. Olivia was a stay-at-home mom in her late twenties when I first met her. She came to see me because she was looking for some tools to help her feel more peaceful and enjoy her young son. She told me she felt enormous stress inside but couldn't figure out why. She had a young, healthy son, a beautiful home, and a loving husband. She knew she had so much to feel grateful for and was confused about where her stress was coming from.

Although she was grateful to be home with her son, she felt that in the process of becoming a stay-at-home mom, she had lost her "Self." She felt deeply unhappy and unfulfilled, and she knew she needed to do something different but had no idea what. Olivia decided to take a step back, turn her attention inward, and as she said, "…think about myself as an individual, a person, separate from my role as a wife and mom."

The way she coped with her stress was by binge eating everything in sight, which set her up for feeling more stressed, which led to more binge eating, followed by guilt for binge eating, which caused more stress and more binge eating, and so on. From the outside, Olivia was a kind, fit, loving, intelligent woman who had it all together. But on the inside, she didn't feel that way.

Like many women, she knew she wasn't depressed, and she was willing to make some changes. She began with a daily ten-minute meditation practice. Olivia noticed quickly that she was beginning to feel different inside. She described it like her "stress threshold" had been raised. Things that would have set her off before didn't seem to bother her as much. She was able to step back a bit more and see what needed to change in her life. She learned how to be with herself and accept the full range of her emotions without needing to numb them through eating. She learned how to work through her feelings and, in the process, slowly kicked her stress eating habit to the curb. She was able to make conscious choices, rather than mindlessly reacting to the stressful moments in her day.

Knowing what brings women like Olivia to meditation workshops is important, but it's also important to understand and dissect what keeps people away. I have a hunch, from talking to many people, that the reasons people aren't meditating are based on false assumptions and beliefs about meditation.

Belief #1   I don't have time to meditate

Saying we don't have time to meditate is like saying we don't have time to brush our teeth. Who can't find five minutes a day to get started? I love what Deepak Chopra says: "If you're too busy to meditate once a day, you need to meditate twice per day." I get it, because I used to say the same thing. The truth was that I didn't want to meditate because I really didn't understand what it was and how it could benefit me. What we often don't realize is that meditation will make us more efficient with our time.

One of my clients, Penny, is a young woman with two young children. She turned to meditation in order to deal with mild anxiety related to working full-time, raising a young family, and being involved in the production of a movie. Penny described how her meditation practice gave her greater clarity and the ability to focus, which in turn gave her more time. She learned how to observe her emotions, as opposed to getting caught up in them and reacting out of frustration. Penny shared how practicing meditation had helped her in a stressful situation at work when she felt an anxiety attack coming on:

> "We had a very stressful meeting at work, a very emotionally charged meeting. In the past I have experienced anxiety attacks, and while I hadn't had one in about ten years, during this meeting I could feel all my symptoms of a panic attack starting, I could feel the war inside bubbling and I started to get light-headed and dizzy, I was shivering but sweating, I started to feel a lump in my throat and heat behind my eyes that promised to be tears. And I knew this is how an anxiety attack starts for me. What now?
>
> So, I left the room, I went to the washroom, I could still feel the impending doom... and then I thought—I'll try to meditate! I found a vacant phone room on the floor and I began to breathe deeply 6...7.... 8...9... I could feel my body start to reset...10... I could think more clearly again...11... and I felt a flood of calm. I know I'm in my sweet spot when I see the indigo circle pulsating just beyond the tip of my nose.... and time passed.... and then I was done.

I went back to the meeting with very different energy and I
could feel my resilience and calm surround me like a bubble.
I was able to give feedback to the manager and interact with
my coworkers in ways that were clear and calm."

Meditation is all about managing our minds and the ripple effects they
have on all aspects of our lives. I have never met anyone who has started
a regular meditation practice and regretted the time spent in cultivating
this habit.

Belief #2   I do yoga, so I don't need to meditate

Before I teach someone how to meditate, I always ask about his or her
previous experience. I often hear "I learned about meditation through yoga."
While I'm a certified meditation and mindfulness teacher, I have very little
experience with yoga other than doing the odd class here and there. As both
yoga and meditation are becoming increasingly popular, I thought I'd ask
one of my fellow meditation teachers who is also a certified yoga teacher
about how meditation and yoga are related and how they are different.

Carla has certifications in Hatha Yoga, Prenatal Yoga, Yin Yoga, Ayurveda
Yoga Therapy and Chinese meridians. She described the difference:

"Meditation is a totally different baby than yoga. What we
refer to as "Yoga" in the west is the Asana or the physical
practice. Dhyana or meditation is also one of the eight limbs
of yoga. While both yoga and meditation are interrelated and
may overlap, the practices, and the nature of the experience
are very different. Meditation typically involves stillness and
more depth and understanding of the mind and its subtleties of
movement. Asana involves the movement of the physical body
and energy moving through the subtle body. As a teacher of
both, I realize that being able to direct and guide the physical
body does not mean skill in directing and guiding the mind.
Just as a meditation teacher trained in guiding the mind is not
by default skilled or trained in guiding the body. I don't think
a class of yoga students would appreciate a meditation teacher

showing up to teach asana so why would it be any different for a yoga teacher expecting to teach a meditation class? A meditation teacher is leading a class through the mind. They need to understand how the mind/brain works, how it labels, judges, categorizes, how the focus wanders, what happens neurologically when we meditate, what happens emotionally, physically, mentally when we meditate. What experiences a person might have in meditation, how to lead a meditation, timing, voice tone, tempo, and guidance is different."

In short, Carla felt strongly that, "I do not think a yoga teacher by default is trained to teach meditation just as I don't think a meditation teacher is by default trained to teach yoga."

Belief #3   I can't meditate, because I can't stop my mind from thinking

I was recently at a workshop and was sitting beside a woman who asked me, "What do you do for a living?" I told her I was a spiritual mentor and meditation teacher. She paused for a moment and then said, "Oh, I've tried to meditate, and I can't do it." When I asked her what she meant by not being able to do it, she expanded, "I can't stop my mind from thinking, and my mind is way too busy, so it never seems to work."

Her response reminded me of the 2010 movie *Eat, Pray, Love* with Julia Roberts. It was based on Elizabeth Gilbert's life when she went on a quest of self-discovery that took her to Italy, India and Bali. Like many of us, Liz thought she had everything in life—a home, a husband, and a successful career—until she found herself at a turning point in her life and was confused about what was important to her.

There's a segment in the movie where Julia Roberts is sitting down to meditate and the first thing she says to herself when she begins is, "Okay, simply empty your mind." I can't tell you how many times I've heard people say they're unable to meditate and the reason they give is because they can't stop their mind from thinking and therefore they can't meditate. This belief is absolutely false. Being able to empty your mind or stop your mind from thinking is not the goal of meditation. We have thousands of thoughts in a day and the point of learning to meditate is learning what to do *when* we have thoughts in meditation, not *if* we have thoughts.

Besides using the movie to point out a common misconception about thoughts during meditation, I wanted to share it because it mirrored my story and one that is becoming increasingly common among women. We possess a deep desire and inner longing to live in alignment with our highest truths and not be stifled by our Small Self and who we believe we should be.

While Julia Roberts flitted off to exotic places to find her Self, I retreated into my cocoon to look inside for the answers. These answers slowly began to emerge as a result of shifting out of survival mode and beginning to tune into myself. With this newfound ability to create a deep state of rest in my body and settle my busy mind, I began to realize my thoughts, feelings, and body were trying to tell me a story I needed to listen to. I was about to discover that learning to deal with my feelings was like opening Pandora's box. Once it was opened, there was no turning back.

Awakening Your Soul

Misbelief: Stress or inner turmoil is part of life and needs to be accepted. You'll feel more peaceful when things like your job, health, or relationships change.
Truth: You have the ability to develop resilience to stress so that the outer circumstances of your life don't harm your physical, emotional, or spiritual health.

Misbelief: Meditation and silence are a luxury and not a necessity.
Truth: In order to create optimal health and connect with your Soul, you need to create space for silence and learn how to master your mind. Your Soul is shy and will only reveal itself in the quiet times in your life when it feels safe.

Misbelief: What you see is what you get. The outer circumstances of your life dictate what is going on inside of you.
Truth: There is a whole world to explore inside you that will lead you to greater peace, fulfillment, meaning happiness, and connection. The inner creates the outer.

Practices/Reflections

1. Carve out at least five minutes a day for meditation or silence. Visit www.bevjanisch.com to receive *A Beginner's Guide to Meditation*. This guide will help you set up a meditation practice and includes an audio recording and a link to my favorite meditation app with thousands of guided meditations.

2. Identify how stress is currently manifesting in your life. Is it impacting your physical or emotional health?

3. If you notice resistance to spending time alone in silence on a daily basis, explore where the resistance is coming from. What stories are you telling yourself about why you can't or shouldn't do it?

CHAPTER 4

Your Awareness is Your Superpower

The outer conditions of a person's life will always be found to reflect their inner beliefs.

—*James Allen*

I grew up as the middle child with two sisters. My sister Nora was three years older than me, and Heather was five years younger. Heather and I would spend hours together playing school down in our unfinished basement—I was the teacher and Heather the student. We had real school desks and a big black chalkboard mounted on the wall. I'm not proud to say that there were occasions I would whip out the ruler to teach Heather a lesson—but what would inevitably happen is that I would be the one being taught a lesson. Heather might have been younger, but she was feistier. After the ruler had been used on me, I'd run off crying to my parents. The response was usually the same: "Quit crying or I'll give you something to cry about."

I learned quickly that running to my parents wasn't the answer. Their response was common in those times and it taught me that my feelings weren't okay to have and they definitely weren't okay to share. The natural thing to do was to shut down my feelings and not allow myself to feel what I was feeling.

Fast forward to my marriage with Mark, where I'm trying to express my feelings about something in our life that is bothering me, such as *Why am I always making sure the kids get to their doctors' appointments and have all their school papers signed?* or *Why do you need to buy a house to renovate on the side when we have two toddlers and you're already never home because you're climbing the corporate ladder and away on golf weekends?* Because I never learned how to deal with my feelings, trying to do so now with Mark usually didn't turn out very well. In the first few years we were together, I'd try and express my feelings and when he didn't seem to understand or validate them, I'd become explosive. We'd get into a big fight and he'd storm off. I found it virtually impossible to rest in this place of turmoil and discomfort, so I'd smooth things over and we'd make up. The problem with this technique was that nothing got resolved. After a number of these embarrassing outbursts, I unconsciously started shifting my approach and tried a more "mature" approach. No arguments, no battles— it looked like peace on the outside, but on the inside it felt like my inner light was slowly going out.

In this new approach, I'd bring up an issue calmly, and Mark would calmly tell me I was unreasonable, and that would be the end of the discussion. I'd shut down because I didn't have the energy for more fighting—the only other way I knew. This was all fueled by my misbelief that I didn't have a right to my feelings in the first place— exactly what I had been telling myself since childhood. This hidden belief prevented me from being vulnerable, which meant that we were going to live like roommates. I was so busy blaming Mark for my explosive outbursts, which over time shifted to the opposite extreme of shutting down, that I didn't see the role that I was playing in it. If Mark would change, I told myself, then I'd be different.

I began to notice this inability to deal with feelings impacted not only my married clients and friends, but also my single ones. It was interesting that while our outer situations may look different, our inner landscapes were the same. We didn't know how to connect and be vulnerable in order to have and/or attract deep meaningful relationships into our lives. We would stay on the surface and either react with extreme emotion or shut down altogether, both of which prevented the deeper layers from being revealed to the other person. These deeper layers relate to our Souls—our hopes, dreams, fears, imperfections, values, and the expression of who we are. We get in the habit of showing our Small Self to others and keeping our Souls hidden. Changing this requires a new way of being and another tool—mindfulness.

Mindfulness teaches us how to be with our thoughts and feelings without exploding or shutting down. It is about learning a whole new way of being. We begin to see that to have a deep connection with someone else, we must first have one with our Self. We realize the change in our lives and relationships that we desire, begins with changing something within ourselves. As Rumi, the Sufi poet said, "Yesterday I was clever, so I wanted to change the world. Today I am wise, so I am changing myself."

What Mindfulness Is Not

For most of my life, I had a much better sense of what it meant to *not* be mindful. And because I believe many women have a similar challenge, I'm going to start by exploring what the absence of mindfulness looks and feels like. Absence of mindfulness happens when we're lost in thoughts about the past or worry about the future. When our minds are someplace other than where our body is. In short, when we're not paying attention.

My daughter Erika taught me what can happen when we're not mindful. Erika was around eight years old when she told me she didn't think that I loved her. I was standing at the kitchen sink doing the dishes and thinking about everything on my to-do list for the rest of the week. She was talking to me about something that happened at school that day, and I was totally zoned out. I wasn't listening to a word she said. What I do remember her saying, because it stopped me in my tracks, was, "Mom, I don't feel that you love me because you don't listen to me." My heart sank. My initial reaction of *How could she say that?* quickly turned into *I'm a horrible mother. My own daughter doesn't feel that I love her. What's wrong with me?* At the time, I hadn't heard about mindfulness as a solution to the issue of being so lost in thought that we tune out the people we love. Mindfulness, then, is presence. And when we can be fully present for and with others, it is the ultimate expression of love. At the time of my conversation with eight-year-old Erika, I definitely needed to learn how to cultivate more presence.

Putting the concept of mindfulness into words in a meaningful way is challenging because the practice is about a way of being rather than something that can be intellectually understood. Still, there are a number of signs that could indicate you might benefit from developing greater mindfulness:

- You notice you are frequently lost in thought.
- You feel stuck in your head and disconnected from your body.
- You either don't know what you're thinking or you over-identify with your thoughts and the stories you tell yourself.
- You have difficulty dealing with your feelings and avoid, numb, or suppress certain feelings.
- You don't pay attention to the little things like doing the laundry, going for a walk, or things occurring in nature.
- You tell yourself that you shouldn't feel or think certain things.
- You judge yourself for what you *do* feel and think.
- You're not aware of how different people and situations leave you feeling inside your body.
- You notice that the little voice in your head is like a bad roommate, always criticizing.
- You're already thinking about the next thing before you're finished with the task at hand.
- You find it hard to concentrate and stay focused on tasks or conversations.

What Mindfulness Is

Mindfulness has its roots in Buddhist meditation and is over 2500 years old. Mindfulness became mainstream when Jon Kabat-Zinn introduced a secular program of mindfulness called Mindfulness-Based Stress Reduction (MBSR) in the 1970s. Mindfulness is one form of meditation that may include a formal sitting practice, as well as a way of being as we go about our day-to-day lives.

Just as the term "meditation" can be confusing and mean different things to different people, "mindfulness" is also open to varying interpretations. The book *Mindfulness in Plain English* by Bhante Gunaratana is a helpful resource to understand mindfulness in general. The author cautions that most of the books written about meditation, including mindfulness, "are written from a point of view that lies squarely within one particular religious or philosophical tradition, and many of the authors have not bothered to point this out" (2011, p. 11). He rightfully identifies that this has created "a real mess."

I would agree. For this reason, when I'm referring to mindfulness, I'm not referring to practices from any particular tradition but rather the basics that seem to be common to all.

Mindfulness in general includes two aspects. One is developing awareness and/or paying attention to what is going on both inside you and around you. This includes being aware of what you're thinking and feeling, and how those thoughts and feelings are showing up in your body. The second component is the *way* in which we're paying attention. In other words, we must pay attention in a way that is kind, loving, and nonjudgmental. In being mindful, we are cultivating the ability to be with whatever arises exactly as it is, without judging it as good or bad, right or wrong. As one of my clients put it, "My inner journey helped me to see that every experience I have been through has shaped me. I no longer see things as good or bad, they are just experiences and all were necessary for me to become who I am today."

Combining a short sitting meditation practice, where we create space for our minds to settle, with the ability to cultivate mindfulness as we move through our days, is a recipe for a new way of being for most of us. As our minds settle, we begin to ask questions such as: *Why do I react the way I do? Why does this situation push my buttons? What is my body telling me about this person or this decision I need to make? How do I manage these uncomfortable feelings? How can I be kinder with myself? What stories am I telling myself? How can I respond with wisdom rather than in anger or frustration?* We're beginning to learn we have a whole world inside us that is colorful, rich, deep, and calling out for our attention.

Mindfulness creates the container to develop an intimate relationship with our inner world, a world that has been sadly neglected and drowned out by the much louder outer world demanding our attention. We are beginning to bring our lives back into balance as we create space for our inner and outer worlds to co-exist in alignment and harmony.

Lynn, a client of mine, was being called to make sense out of the feeling that something was missing in her life. She was a lively, charismatic, and cheerful yoga teacher, who found herself at the age of sixty in quite a funk. She couldn't understand why, because she had a great childhood, a close family and many successes in her life. Her husband would ask, "What's the matter with you?" and she couldn't respond because she had no idea. Lynn explained, "As I began meditation and practiced mindfulness, I became aware of my feelings. I noticed the ups and downs in the relationship with my husband. I just knew I couldn't ignore it any longer. We would be sitting at the kitchen table together, sharing a meal and not talking to each other. I felt like I wasn't being heard when I tried to share something, so I just quit talking altogether."

She began to realize that she had been blaming her husband for her unhappiness and that she needed to make some changes within herself. "I realized that I wasn't going to change Tim, so I was going to need to change myself."

She described how she had become "tired, bitchy, and negative" and knew that was not who she was. Mindfulness helped her see things she hadn't been aware of and she began to understand her feelings. Rather than focusing on Tim, she began to ask, "What do I need to change within myself to get my joy back?"

Lynn started to see that her husband was the scapegoat for what wasn't working in her life. "It's like you're mad at him because you're mad at yourself. I thought if he'd be different then I'd be happy."

As soon as she began to take responsibility for her own happiness and feelings, everything seemed to shift and move in a different direction. "It was a light bulb moment for me that changed everything. As I began to get happier within myself, I began to open up with Tim and then he began to change as well." Lynn noticed that in response to her changes that he became kinder and more accepting and understanding, and they began connecting and sharing again. "I realized that if you're not feeling connected with yourself, it's pretty hard to be connected in your relationships."

This is where mindfulness comes in. We learn how to be with our thoughts and feelings in a way that creates space for wisdom. One of the most common things I hear from women is that they have no idea how to deal with their thoughts, the stories they tell themselves, or their feelings. It's like our thoughts and feelings are out-of-control children who are creating havoc. They demand attention and yet the attention we give them is most often negative. One woman put it this way: "When I began practicing mindfulness and got curious about my feelings and behaviors, I began to unearth what was really going on. The way I treated those around me was a reflection of how I treated myself. If I could not accept myself, then I could not accept others around me. I started to understand why I acted in ways I wasn't proud of, like being unkind, selfish and reactive. As I learned how to look a bit deeper into why I was reacting this way, I could see that I didn't know how to deal with hurt, shame, and fear. Mindfulness taught me how to deal with all of my feelings. It was amazing how that shift changed me and all of my relationships."

As we develop our capacity to live more mindfully, we learn how to feel more fully and deeply, and we spend way less time stuck in our heads and lost in thought. We begin to feel all our feelings. We notice our thoughts and the stories we tell ourselves, and we gain skill in determining whether there is any truth in them or whether they're just automatic recordings based on misbeliefs. As we pay more attention to our surroundings, we begin to notice the water on our faces in the shower, the clouds in the sky and the wind on our cheeks when we are out for a walk. We notice how our body feels either expanded or constricted when we're around certain people. We have more and more moments in the day when we catch ourselves lost in thought about the past or the present. We notice how much of our thinking energy is creative, fresh, and new—and how much is old and stale.

Mindfulness enables us to not only pay attention, but to pay attention in a kind way. This way of being enables us to move through life with greater ease, as we appreciate the times when life is smooth and things are going well, and we are open to the times when life is challenging us. The ultimate test of mindfulness came when my nephew Andy died tragically at a young age. Andy and I had been very close, and his death had a deep and lasting impact on me. Looking back, I realized having the ability to be with my feelings in a way that honored them was a big gift. I allowed myself to feel all my grief. I felt the pain fully and created space for that pain and hurt in my life. In the past I might have tried to suppress, deny, or numb the sadness, but my mindfulness practice enabled me to lovingly embrace my grief, which over time allowed it to soften.

Creating a New Way of Being

As our minds settle and we develop a new relationship with our thoughts and feelings, we begin to see the effects of these inner changes in the outer aspects of our lives. We develop a physical, emotional, and spiritual resilience that begins to heal us from the inside out. I have experienced this healing power of meditation and mindfulness in my own life and I've seen it in the lives of the women that I work with. Chronic stress that had been wreaking havoc in women's hormones and health is replaced by a nourishing way of being. Women begin to experience less anxiety and depression because they aren't stuffing down their feelings or ignoring the messages from their Soul that something in their life is out of alignment.

As we become more aware of our thoughts and create space for our feelings, we begin to transform. We no longer tell ourselves we shouldn't feel a certain way. We also don't feel the same need to turn to others for validation of our feelings. While being validated can be a beautiful thing, we must learn to create space for our feelings, even when others don't necessarily understand them or feel the same way. When we accept our feelings no matter what, we allow our feelings to exist in our relationships without pushing them aside. This change within us creates a ripple effect in those relationships. Learning to be with our Self is the first step towards learning to be with someone else in a way that nourishes our Souls within our relationships.

One of my clients, Betty, put it this way:

> "What I noticed when I began to practice meditation and mindfulness was that I had never allowed myself to feel what I was feeling. I just buried everything and I didn't want to express my feelings because I didn't want to appear weak. I saw my mom as weak and I didn't want to be like her. I had a lot of stuff going on inside that I felt I couldn't let out. Because I didn't allow myself to feel what I was feeling and tried to stuff it down it came out in really awful ways especially towards my kids and husband. As I began to allow myself to feel it, I began to see more clearly where it was coming from. It was like a miracle. As I allowed myself to feel it and understand what

it was telling me, it just went away. The feelings just moved through me and weren't getting stuck anymore."

When I brought this new mindfulness dance into my relationship with Mark, it changed how disagreements and conflicts played out. I would notice my anger, allow myself to feel it, and give it space to be there. I might even decide to label it by saying to myself, *This is anger and this is what it feels like in my body.* While I might be tempted to push the anger away because it didn't feel comfortable, I knew resisting it would only make it stick around longer. I might have wanted to reach for a cookie or a carton of ice cream to deal with the discomfort, but instead I got curious about how the feeling of anger felt inside my body. I began to watch it and follow it without getting all caught up in it. I then noticed it would start to dissolve. Generally speaking, feelings we don't try to suppress, usually only last a few seconds.

Once the feeling had dissipated, I would tell Mark I was angry. He then would defensively reply that I was over-reacting, irrational, and shouldn't feel that way. But instead of over-reacting or shutting down, I allowed myself to feel what I was feeling. I confidently and kindly responded, "This situation triggered this anger in me. I'm not saying it's your fault, but I am saying that I feel this way and I have a right to these feelings." I noticed that because I stopped blaming him, his defensiveness seemed to subside. I was transforming my relationship with my feelings and in the process, I was also transforming the way Mark and I communicated and dealt with conflict.

The same holds true for our thoughts and the stories that we tell ourselves. Mindfulness helps us learn how to observe our thoughts and the stories without believing them or getting swept away by them. As we begin to observe our thoughts, we begin to see and feel the difference between the thoughts that are arising from our Small Self as opposed to the thoughts that are flowing from our Soul and our connection with an intelligent universe. This difference came up continually as I was writing this book. I've had endless Small Self thoughts telling me such things as: *Who are you to write this book? It's so boring. Nobody wants to read this. What a waste of time. You're not smart or expert enough.* These thoughts and stories are there but they aren't the ones I'm going to listen to. I smile at them and then carry on because I've learned to listen to the thoughts and ideas that are coming from my Soul, which is saying: *You are meant to share this transformation in service of others who may be struggling; you are worthy; you are enough; what you have to say matters; one day maybe your children and grandchildren and great grandchildren will read this and they'll know who you were; don't die with a story left in you.*

As we become aware of how our Small Self and Soul come together to form our sense of who we are, we can make a choice. We are no longer victims of our minds. Rather, we are creators of the life that we want, and that aligns with the needs of our Souls. As we do that, we expand our consciousness and begin to walk through the world with confidence and an awareness of who we are and what we need to live in alignment with our highest Self. Mindfulness teaches us to be at peace with both our Small Self and our Soul, while simultaneously letting us choose to feed those aspects of ourselves that we want to expand, while accepting the other aspects with patience, kindness, and love.

What You Focus on Expands

How do we cultivate more nourishing thoughts and feelings in our lives, while accepting that at times we have thoughts that trigger uncomfortable and constricted feelings we'd rather not have?

I learned the answer to this question the hard way a few years ago when I was training for a triathlon and was out for a cycle. I was always a bit freaked out on this particular light bike because of the clip-in pedals and the feeling of vulnerability its skinny tires gave me when they seemed to float and drift with the slightest shift in my attention.

It was a beautiful day with the sun shining as I cruised along the highway heading west towards the mountains. I could see the snow-capped peaks as the rolling hills stretched out before me. I felt amazing and had this total sense of freedom as I cycled along.

Mark was way ahead of me, and as I settled into a nice rhythm, I heard a loud truck coming up behind me. I turned my head to glance behind me, thinking to myself, *just don't go in the ditch.* You can probably guess what happened…I went down hard in the ditch.

My head hit the pavement with a smack and my body slammed into the road. Fortunately, beyond being stunned and having a bruise the size of a huge watermelon on my leg, I was okay.

What did that experience teach me about the way the mind works? It taught me that our minds are manifesting machines and that we must always focus on what we *do* want rather than what we *don't* want. The mind doesn't understand what it means to *not* want something. So by saying I didn't want to go in the ditch, that's exactly where I was going to go.

It's amazing when you begin to notice your thoughts, how much we tend to focus on what we don't want to happen or how we don't want to feel. We don't want a bad marriage, or to feel unhappy or be afraid, and yet our mind often focuses on what we need to do to avoid something negative, as opposed to attracting something positive.

Whether you want to hit the fairway (and not the sand trap) when you're golfing, feel connected (rather than disconnected), feel happy (as opposed to *I don't want to be unhappy*) or simply not fall off your bike, it's vital that you focus on what you want *more* of. A popular 21st century parable attributed to Native Americans known as "Which one do you feed" is the story of a grandfather teaching his grandson about the inner conflict that many of us experience:

"A fight is going on inside me", he said to the boy.
"It is a terrible fight and it is between two wolves.
One is anger, envy, sorrow, regret, greed, arrogance, self-pity, guilt, resentment, inferiority, lies, false pride, superiority, self-doubt, and ego.
The other is joy, peace, love, hope, serenity, humility, kindness, benevolence, empathy, generosity, truth, compassion, and faith. This same fight is going on inside of you—and inside of every other person, too."
The grandson thought about it for a minute and then asked his grandfather,
"Which wolf will win?"
The old chief replied,
"The one you feed."

Breaking the Negativity Habit

As my ability to observe my thoughts and feelings grew, I noticed I had a lot of negative thoughts. I tended to gravitate to the things that weren't working in my life, even though I knew I was supposed to be feeding the other wolf. The problem was that I didn't know *how* to do that. How exactly are we supposed to feed the wolf that we want more of?

I was beginning to see memes about gratitude everywhere and while I kept hearing how powerful it was, I didn't understand why it was so important. I thought it seemed a bit corny and noticed I would often roll my eyes reading this stuff. Deep down, I felt embarrassed that I didn't feel more grateful. This created a little struggle inside of me. I knew I *should* feel more grateful because I had so much to feel grateful for—and yet my mind always seemed to drift towards what I was lacking or what wasn't working in my life. Just like the parable I shared about the two wolves, I had one that focused on the negative, even while I wanted to feed the other wolf of gratitude and appreciation. What I came to learn was that I wasn't alone in my tendency towards being on guard and focusing on the negative. I was relieved to discover that being negative is actually "normal" and that it didn't mean that I was ungrateful or had some deep, dark problem. Dr. Rick Hanson, a psychologist, talks about this in his book *Buddha's Brain: The Practical Neuroscience of Happiness, Love & Wisdom*, where he refers to it as the "negativity bias." We are hardwired towards negativity because our very survival depends on it. As he explains, "That's because it's the negative experiences, not the positive ones, that have generally had the most impact for survival" (2009, p. 40).

This would explain an experience I had when I recently spoke to a group of corporate leaders about meditation. Part of the practice for this group was to provide the speakers an evaluation after the talk and rate them based on a scale of one to five. Following the talk, I was told I got mostly fives, a few fours and one three. My immediate focus and energy went into processing the fact that I got a three, which of course felt very negative to me. Most of the people had rated the talk very high and yet I became almost obsessed with the three, which left me feeling negative about something that was actually positive. Every person in that group except one thought my talk was awesome, and yet all I could focus on was that one person who thought it was average. My mind was stuck on that three as if my life depended on it. It was comforting to know my response was normal—albeit not helpful.

How do we counteract our natural tendency towards negativity? Like all mindfulness practices, we cultivate more of what we do want rather than suppressing, denying, or giving ourselves a hard time over what we don't want. The more we resist the negativity, the more it persists. Understanding the concept that what we focus on is what expands is helpful on our journey towards cultivating a healthier and happier mind, which means a healthier and happier life.

Rick Hanson talks about a practice called "**taking in the good**," which I have found helpful in counteracting the negativity bias. It's like a gratitude practice on steroids. As you're going about your day and noticing the things that feel positive or that you're grateful for, pause and let the experience sink in. Hanson says to "savor the experience" (p. 69). The longer we can pause and the more deeply we can feel the experience, the better. Try it the next time you get or give a hug, hold a baby, see a flower, feel the sun on your face, take a bubble bath, or are smiled at by someone at the grocery store…pause and savor the experience.

As we're noticing, pausing, and savoring the experiences in our lives that feel good, we're building new neuropathways in our brain. We now understand that the pathways that fire together wire together, which means we are developing a new habit of noticing and taking in the positive. I want to stress here that this practice isn't about being positive all the time. There is an important difference between focusing on the little moments of gratitude and appreciation and telling ourselves that we have to *think positive*. In fact, this whole "I've got to think positive" thing is really quite problematic. Denying what we're thinking or feeling is never the answer. It creates a battle within us. On the surface it looks like the two wolves, but it's really just the one: one wolf thinking negative thoughts on one hand and the same wolf telling us *not* to think the negative thoughts on the other hand. See? It's all the same wolf.

So what do we do instead with the negative thoughts? We notice them, bow to them, and allow them to be there without judgment or resistance. As mindfulness is teaching us, when we accept them without judgment or resistance, they will move on through us. And the whole time we're doing this; we're building new habits—in particular, the habit of being kind to ourselves, no matter what. By accepting our thoughts without getting attached or over-identifying with them, along with consciously looking for opportunities in our day to savor the good, many of us will learn an entirely new way of being.

Bookend Your Days

When I returned to Calgary, leaving Mark in Phoenix, I had many mornings—a couple of months' worth—of waking up alone. We had been married for more than thirty years and other than a couple of weeks here and there, we had never been apart for that long. I woke up most mornings with some pretty negative thoughts whirling around in my head. *"What is wrong with me? I feel I need to be alone, but I'm miserable alone. What am I going to do with my life now that I've turned it all upside down? How could I do this to Mark?"* And when I say whirling, I mean whirling. I seemed to go around in circles with the same thoughts and the same outcome—me feeling confused about why I felt I needed to make these changes in the first place.

But the universe decided to be kind to me and drew my attention to Louise Hay's book, *The Essential Louise Hay Collection*. As I read the following section, I had that inner excitement that happens when you read something that is screaming your name:

> "What is the first thing you say in the morning when you wake up? We all have something we say almost every day. Is it positive or negative? I can remember when I used to awaken in the morning and say with a groan, "OH GOD, ANOTHER DAY." And that is exactly the sort of day I would have, one thing after another going wrong. Now when I awaken and before I open my eyes, I thank the bed for a good night's sleep. After all, we have spent the whole night together in comfort. Then with my eyes still closed, I spend about ten minutes just being thankful for all the good in my life. I program my day a bit, affirming that everything will go well and that I will enjoy all of it. This is before I get up and do my morning meditations or prayers" (2013, p. 104).

I was determined to give this new plan a try. Beginning my day with a new mindset made a big change in my life. Rather than ruminating on all the ways my life felt like a train wreck, I'd shift my mind to noticing all the little things I had going for me. I began to understand how unruly and destructive our untrained minds often are. For the majority of my life, my mind literally had a mind of its own and would tell me all sorts of stories, which for the most part were quite toxic. Now I was saying *"no more"*, and I was beginning to take my mind back. I had more power over it than I ever realized.

I was also beginning to realize that how we end our day and what is going through our mind before we drift off to sleep is equally important. I decided to end my days with a simple gratitude practice. When I first began this gratitude practice, it felt a bit forced and more like an intellectual exercise. I'd pull out my journal at bedtime and make a list of all the things I was grateful for during the day. At first, I didn't really feel anything, and it felt mechanical. But I stuck with it. Before long, I noticed how I was bringing that increased awareness of things I was grateful for into the day. I'd notice things I hadn't really paid attention to, such as a sunset, a cup of coffee, a call from my friend. I realized a shift was happening inside me. I was beginning to be more appreciative.

To give you an idea of what a mindfulness plan might look like, I'll give you a quick overview of mine. Every morning I open my eyes and focus on gratitude. I then spend a few minutes grounding myself in some inspirational reading to remind myself that I am a spiritual being and the universe has my back. I enjoy books with short inspirational passages based on ancient spiritual texts or teachers. This fills my mind and Soul with all sorts of nourishing ideas and reminds me that I am an expression of something much larger than myself. This sets the stage for a few minutes in meditation, which I then wrap up with prayer. For me, meditation allows me to be open to hearing the messages from the universe, and prayer is like talking to the creative life force. I seal the deal with setting an intention for the day. My intentions usually focus on ways I can nourish my health and my relationships, and the difference I want to make in the world.

At the end of my day, I either journal about gratitude or do a heart-centered gratitude practice. I often listen to soothing meditation music and make sure all my devices are out of my bedroom. Before I drift off to sleep, if there is some question I have or something I am confused about, I visualize turning it over to the universe for help or to provide me with guidance. I plant lots of questions into the creative medium of the intelligent life force. The answers seem to arrive in the most surprising and yet ordinary ways—books, songs, conversations, insights, "aha" moments, and people.

When I was building these simple practices into my day, I began to experience some big shifts in how I experienced my life. I could sense that my Small Self was taking up less space and my Soul was coming into the forefront. And yet, I also felt something more needed my attention. With my newfound awareness, I noticed resentment surfacing. Even though I was meditating regularly, practicing gratitude and prayer, and bookending my days with good inspiring stuff, I could feel that resentment simmering. Mindfulness had increased my awareness to the point that I couldn't ignore it any longer. Why was I still blaming Mark for so much? Why did I feel like I had ice around my heart? My Soul needed to express itself more fully, and yet there was something inside me that was making it hard to reach. Apparently, the next step on my journey would be to face the anger and resentment lurking inside me. I was being called to gain an understanding about where this toxic energy came from so I could transform it and finally connect with my Soul.

Awakening Your Soul

Misbelief: Your feelings and emotions are good/bad, right/wrong. You're supposed to only feel the good ones.
Truth: Feelings are a source of wisdom and you're meant to feel all of them. When you numb or suppress uncomfortable feelings, you numb and suppress *all* feelings.

Misbelief: It's abnormal to have negative thinking.
Truth: Your mind has a natural tendency towards negativity. Certain practices will shift your negativity and help you create a new way of being.

Misbelief: The conscious and subconscious beliefs you inherited from your family and cultural views about women don't impact your life.

Truth: Absolutely every aspect of your life including your career, money, relationships, health, and happiness are impacted by your beliefs. Some you are aware of and others you are not. Change your beliefs and your life will change.

Practices/Reflections

1. Understand what mindfulness is and the qualities that make up mindfulness by doing the Mindfulness Quiz (https://greatergood. berkeley.edu/quizzes/take_quiz/mindfulness) on The Greater Good website. Identify areas for improvement in your daily life.

2. Develop a plan to "bookend" your days with inspiring activities such as gratitude, meditation, prayer, and inspiring reading. Write out the plan in your journal.

3. What beliefs from your childhood are you carrying around with you? Are they helpful or limiting? Examples might include: you're selfish if you care for yourself; you are meant to be seen and not heard; you're not good enough; it's okay to only have certain feelings; your voice doesn't matter; you're not important; you're not smart enough; women are meant to be a certain way.

CHAPTER 5

The Gifts of Anger and Resentment

"If you're not full of love, what are you full of?"

— Loraine

I vividly remember the day thirty-one years ago, when we brought our daughter Erika home from the hospital. It was a beautiful spring day and a welcome relief from a long, cold winter in Estevan, Saskatchewan. Mark and I had been living there for a couple of years before Erika was born. A few months after we'd been married, Mark had come home from work one day and announced, "I got transferred to Estevan and we need to pack up and be there within the next month." The tears started streaming down my face. I had just graduated with my degree in nursing a few months before and had started working at the hospital on a general surgery unit. The transfer meant I would have to give up my job and live in a small town with no job, family, friends, or anything to do. I would be leaving Calgary, Alberta, a city I loved with close to one million people—and move to a small town of ten thousand strangers. There was no real discussion—it was simply presented as what needed to happen. Still, I had this unsettled feeling inside and a whisper of a little voice that came ever so faintly from someplace deep inside: *What if I don't want to move? What about my career? Why is your career more important than mine?* And then I heard a response from what I now know was my Small Self: *Don't be so selfish. You'll make it work. Mark makes more money so that means his job is more important.* And so I resigned from my nursing job and off we went.

Several months later in Estevan, I landed my dream job and began working at the local hospital developing a day program for seniors. My job was deeply fulfilling as I used my gifts and passion for working with seniors and had the opportunity to create something new from the ground up. It was a new program to support seniors to live in their homes as long as possible, and I loved the challenge and opportunity to make a difference. Mark was working as an engineer and was gaining experience to further his career in the oil and gas industry. And then I got pregnant.

The day we brought Erika home, everything in my life changed again. I walked into our house with this little, vulnerable, dependent human being and thought, *Now what? What do I do with this little person who is now totally my responsibility?* As I grappled with the uncertainty, the unknown, and the outright fear, Mark turned and said, "I think I'm going to cut the grass. It's looking long and I haven't had a chance since spending so much time at the hospital." I kept my mouth shut, but I could hear myself shouting inside, *You're going outside to cut the grass without any consideration for the fact that we have a brand new baby?* As blind as I was to it, a pattern had begun to show up in my life. *Why wasn't I using my voice? What was I afraid of? How was I meant to be in these important roles in my life—first as daughter, then as wife and mother—without losing my Self?*

As Mark left to cut the grass, it hit me like a ton of bricks. I knew when I woke up the next day, my life would be totally different and his would be only somewhat so. He would wake up and go to his job because as the person who made more money, his career was primary and mine secondary. He would make plans for his business trips and golf games that were necessary for networking so he could fulfill his primary role, in the family, which was to provide for our family. I, on the other hand, would wake up and my sense of freedom as I had known it even a few days before, would have vanished.

Every decision I made for the next thirty years would be based on my roles and my beliefs about what it meant to be a "good" wife, mother, daughter, friend, and human being. When I'd make decisions based on what I needed to do to be a "good" person rather than on my Soul's needs and deep values, I would deposit resentment and bitterness into my internal bank without even realizing it. These beliefs led me from saying, "yes" to moving to a small town without discussion, to saying "yes" to a place in Phoenix that I didn't want.

Sue Monk Kidd, who wrote *The Dance of The Dissident Daughter: A Woman's Journey from Christian Tradition to the Sacred Feminine,* referred to this role as the "secondary partner." She put it this way, "In the model of the secondary partner, the woman may run things at home and have her career, her pursuits, and her quests, but there is a graduation of power in the relationship" (2016, p. 64). Like many women, I subconsciously blamed my husband for the fact that I would just go along and not rock the boat. I had a sense that he had greater freedom, and the leading role while I had the supporting one. Even though it appeared to outsiders that we were "equal," when it came right down to it, we weren't. And this inequality, subtle and difficult to spot, was causing ice to slowly form around my heart.

I discovered I had total freedom to create my life and make decisions, but only as long as it fit within the supporting role. Within that secondary container, I did the best I could to lead a satisfying and happy life as I balanced my home life with my Soul work of being a nurse. I returned to school and pursued part-time studies to earn a Master's degree in Nursing. I had a meaningful life and had many happy, fulfilling years living as a spouse within the rules and expectations outlined by my upbringing, society, my misbeliefs, and the inherited ways of being from all the women who had gone before me.

I lived that role of a secondary partner until I found myself at the top of Mount Kilimanjaro at the age of fifty with a deep yearning to not live a secondary life anymore. While I had gained a deep gratitude, love, and wisdom from those fifty years, I had also accumulated anger and resentment that were turning into bitterness without fully understanding why. Much of this bitterness was directed towards Mark, even though I knew he was the kindest, most loving man I had ever known. While I had no idea at the time, it was my Soul speaking and saying, *You've lived in someone else's shadow for too long. You're not meant to always compromise yourself in order to go along and not rock the boat. You have a voice inside that you're stifling, and it needs to be expressed. You need to step out of the shadows and into the light. You need to live your life based on your own terms. The person who makes more money doesn't run the show.*

Without realizing how I got there, I had arrived in midlife with layers of anger and resentment that began in childhood and then slowly, gradually, and insidiously built up until I was at the point where I felt toxic inside. I was being called to change, but I didn't understand why, and I most certainly had no idea how.

This anger and resentment had been brewing for years, and because I didn't know how to release it, I tried to ignore it. I didn't allow myself to feel the anger because with such a fortunate life, what could I possibly be angry about? I had been very good at telling myself I shouldn't feel a certain way. I was also good at putting myself in other people's shoes, which meant I was actually better at understanding their feelings than my own. This created the perfect storm for keeping me stuck and denying the anger and resentment I was feeling.

As my skill at mindfulness began to take hold, I began to realize I was allowed to have my feelings and that they were actually a source of wisdom rather than something to be denied and suppressed. I opened myself to exploring the wisdom in my resentment and became more curious.

I learned that I had always come at forgiveness for both others and myself from an intellectual perspective. After all, I was an academic at heart. I didn't realize there was a difference between processing things at the level of the head as compared to the deeper level of the heart. I was putting bandages on symptoms and hoping that it would be enough to make the feelings dissipate. But the truth was that I had no idea there were other ways of being because the anger and resentment festering beneath the surface had become normal for me.

Our Collective Dance with Resentment

When I begin working with a woman, I have her fill out a get-acquainted form where she paints a picture of what is working and not working in her life. I don't recall one woman ever writing down that they felt anger and resentful, and yet when we begin to explore it further, the majority of women score an eight out of ten in terms of feeling anger and resentment towards others or disappointment with themselves. Beneath the smiles and masks we show to the world, there are a lot of women suffering as anger and resentment bubbles away just below the surface, waiting to erupt.

That anger and resentment is like the elephant in the room. It's unmistakeably present and has a huge impact in our lives, and yet we don't talk about it. It is like a silent epidemic amongst women. This unresolved anger festers in us and impacts every cell in our body. It not only leaves us feeling lousy, it triggers the stress response that elevates our stress hormones and impacts both our physical and emotional health.

I was working away on my computer in Starbucks between meetings one day, when a young woman sitting next to me looked over and smiled. "You seem to be busy working away on something. Are you a writer?" I was a bit surprised because I thought I was giving off the *don't talk to me now vibe*. I told her I was working on a book about awakening a woman's Soul. With a knowing look on her face, she began to tell me her story. She shared how she was getting married to a great guy in a few months and that she knew how lucky she was because he was kind, stable, and the perfect balance for her. He had been really great and supported her financially with a business she wanted to start up. She went on to say, "I'm a bit confused though…for the last couple of years I feel like I'm slowly losing myself in this relationship. I know it's the best thing ever to marry this man, because he is so good for me, but I'm afraid that I'm going to lose my freedom. I feel like my Soul is withering a little. I don't know how to be in this relationship and not give up my gypsy nature. Whenever I talk to him about it and my need to travel, he reminds me that we need to be cautious because of the money. And although I agree with him, I feel like he's so good about the money that I can't really say anything. I know it will all work out though. I just wish I didn't feel this way with my wedding coming up." As she talked, there was a sense of hesitation in her voice, as if she was trying to talk herself into her decision and how great it was going to be.

I knew this dance all too well. The challenge is that we often can't see the dance when we're in the middle of it. We aren't aware of the beliefs that leave us feeling that we are secondary partners, or that our freedom is being threatened, or that our Souls aren't thriving. We can't see the role money is playing in the power imbalance in our relationships. Many of us don't know how to be in relationships that create space for us to maintain the "I" and not get lost in the "we". As a result, we build up what I call a garden-variety anger and resentment—a sense of impending "doom" that signifies that we're at risk of slowly losing ourselves. The build-up is slow and often invisible. It's similar to the nineteenth century myth that tells us when a frog is placed in a pot of boiling water, it will immediately try to escape, but if it is placed in cold water that slowly heats up, it will remain there until it's too late. While the story has been scientifically debunked, it perfectly illustrates what *does* happen to many women. A slow, gradual giving up on our Souls in favor of our familiar and comfortable way of being that we don't even realize we're doing—until we reach the crisis point of Soul hunger. My new friend in Starbucks was powerfully describing this, and yet she wasn't aware that she would have to change *herself* in order to be different in her relationship. She was waiting for her partner to change, when in fact she was the one who needed to challenge her beliefs about money and power.

I've observed from both my own life and from working with many women that there are certain ways of being based on misbeliefs that create the conditions for anger, resentment, and disappointment to brew:

- The belief that our worth is often tied to how much we give, help, and sacrifice ourselves for others.
- The role that money plays in who holds the "power."
- The tendency to stifle our voices.
- Our belief that other people's needs are more important than our own.
- The tendency to compromise the needs of our Souls for our roles and other people's goals.
- The inherited collective beliefs and wounds from the women who have gone before us that have defined what it means to be a "good" woman.
- The belief that we are responsible for other people's happiness.
- The tendency to put on a happy face when we're fuming inside.
- Our tendency to shut down and/or disown our feelings.

It's no wonder women feel a great deal of anger and resentment inside when we believe that we don't matter, that other people's needs are more important than our own, and that we're meant to be invisible, quiet, kind, accommodating, and helpful as we sacrifice ourselves for others. Although our anger and resentment are understandable and for many justified, keeping the cycle going robs us of our peace of mind—and it starves our Souls.

For many years, a friend of mine named Becky wondered where all her anger and resentment came from. Becky did everything that was expected of her. She went to university, got married, had a child, and tried desperately to be a good wife, mother, and teacher. From the outside, she was a beautiful and charismatic woman who had a kind and gentle way about her. On the inside, however, it was a different story. This is how Becky described it:

> "I grew up in a family where the only acceptable emotion was happiness. I learned quickly to hide any sadness, fear, anger, or anxiety that I felt by convincing myself that I was wrong to feel that way. I learned quickly how to adapt to the unspoken message that my job was to please others. I learned to be quiet, small, and invisible in an environment of anxiety, uncertainty, and fear. I learned the best way to disguise all emotions was by smiling or hiding. I was conditioned to deny my own voice and feelings so that I could be accepted at home. I closed myself off from my own intuition and what I wanted and needed. As a result, I spent most of my life searching for acceptance and looking outward for approval. When the resentment and anger would surface, I would eat and eat. I spent decades in relationships trying to look and be what I thought was the right way to be. Rage and anger began to surface as I reacted to a lifetime of having my needs silenced."

In order to transform these feelings, women who are awakening are being called to create new ways of being that honor our feelings, needs, voices, and the right to express ourselves fully in all aspects of our lives. These feelings of anger, resentment, and losing ourselves are signs we need to make some fundamental changes in our lives. We need to be willing to look at the sources of this anger and resentment, to own the part we play in perpetuating them, and then to courageously make some changes to shift the patterns.

When we begin to respect ourselves more and allow ourselves to have our feelings and needs honored, it acts as a huge catalyst to change the patterns in our relationships. Learning how to respond in a way that honors both ourselves and the other person in a relationship when our buttons are being pushed, is an important place to start.

When Your Buttons Get Pushed

As with most things in life, the most effective approach is preventing problems before they arise. This is especially true when it comes to understanding the dance with anger and resentment and how it builds. In women it often escalates because we don't know how to handle the moments when our buttons get pushed in a way that builds wisdom, growth, and maturity. We are most often triggering our Small Self and blaming the other person for all the things they've done to us. We often get to a point where we're lashing out and don't fully understand why.

As I began reading *A Course in Miracles,* a self-study guide aiming to assist people with spiritual transformation, a lesson jumped out at me that helped me understand what is going on when our buttons get pushed. The lesson was, "I am never upset for the reason I think" (2007, p. 8). I noticed that when people were pushing my buttons, I was so busy focused on what the other person needed to do to change, I didn't see how it was actually me who needed to change. The lesson doesn't say we're not meant to feel what we feel, rather that we need to look a bit deeper to understand what the real trigger is so we can learn and grow from it.

These buttons are part of our Soul's sensor and are warning signs to pay attention as changes may be in order. We're so busy focusing our attention on the button itself that we don't learn the deeper lesson. For example, when I arrived home from the hospital with Erika and Mark left to cut the grass without a care in the world, a button was pushed in me. He wasn't intentionally pushing the button, but because I didn't know to look for my lesson, it became fertilizer for anger and resentment. I was meant to learn how to use my voice—not by blaming Mark, but by sharing how I was feeling. I had stifled my voice and my needs and then blamed Mark for pushing my buttons.

The next time someone or something pushes your buttons, pause and say, "I'm never upset for the reason I think." This will remind you to look for the deeper reason, which is most likely related to some misbelief you have.

The issue isn't about the money, the chores, the household responsibilities, or any other surface thing. It's about something deeper that you have come to believe. For example, one day Mark came out of the kitchen waving the almost empty coffee pot at me. This immediately pushed my buttons and I got really mad. Why? It wasn't about the coffee pot that I hadn't refilled. It was about my underlying belief that I wasn't good enough and had disappointed him. Such a stupid thing really, but most things that push our buttons are stupid things and that's why "I'm never upset for the reason I think."

I came up with a practice to help women when they notice their buttons getting pushed. We remind ourselves to **pause, connect, honor**. This three-step process helps us stop before we react out of anger or just shut down. We pause to take a few breaths and notice how we're feeling in our body; we allow ourselves to settle down before we attempt to understand why our buttons got pushed. We then connect with our Self and look for the deeper reason that we got triggered. Once we have created space to pause and connect with our deeper truths, we are able to honor what we need from a place of wisdom. It is through this process that we may learn we need to change something within ourselves. Perhaps we need better boundaries recognizing that we have a right to consider our own needs or wants. Or we may need to learn how to say "no" when it feels right or "yes" to things we need without feeling guilty. Often we need to learn how to deal with and share our feelings in a way that doesn't result in us lashing out or shutting down. Regardless of the situation, we learn that we are meant to gain wisdom and not blame someone else.

Spontaneous Release of Anger and Resentment

When we deal with shifting things within ourselves or questioning our misbeliefs, we show up differently in relationships and the underlying anger and resentment often disappears spontaneously or is used to fuel our growth. One of my clients, Kim, would get really angry when her husband made decisions with which she felt she needed to go along. She would storm off thinking, "He's a total jerk and control freak. Everything has to be his way. His routines, his structure, his decisions." She found herself continually reacting and wasn't aware to look deeper for how she was meant to be different. In the meantime, her husband assumed Kim didn't care because she always just went along, When Kim became aware of how she was contributing to the situation and realized she wasn't a victim, she began to change. Kim explained, "As I began to see that I was blaming my husband for everything because of my willingness to go along with him, things changed with him. I began to express my feelings more and he began to respect my opinions and me more. Now I feel we have a more respectful and loving relationship. Not because he changed, but because I changed."

The all too common dance of anger and resentment goes like this: You feel unhappy about something or someone in your life and you feel that if they were different, then you'd be happier. You try and change them in order for you to feel better, and when they don't change or don't change enough, you feel angry and resentful. This anger and resentment then either simmers inside or becomes the fuel for explosive outbursts towards the other person, who is often left wondering: *where did all this come from?* You then feel bad about yourself and guilty because of the way you reacted. Now you're both ticked off at the other person and disappointed or angry with yourself. The dance continues until we create a new one based on the realization that *we* are the only people we can change.

I vividly remember the day I had a spontaneous release of a great deal of buried anger, resentment, and blame that I had been carrying around towards Mark for many years. I was in the middle of reading the book *Tune In* by Sonia Choquette, when a Facebook post from Sonia showed up on my feed one Saturday morning. I had been wrestling with making some decisions in my life about how I wanted to move forward. *Do I want to go back to school, write a book, go on a retreat, or explore ways to be of service?* And most importantly, *What was keeping me stuck from moving forward? What was I afraid of?* There was something in me that needed and wanted a deeper and fuller expression of myself in the world, and there was also something in me that held me back. I did something completely out of character for me and signed up through Facebook for a half-hour intuitive reading with Sonia. Compounding my own inner resistance to change, I was getting a sense from Mark that he was also resistant to me moving forward in a different direction. After all, my decision to come out of retirement was having a big impact on him and how he thought our life should unfold.

My heart was pounding as I hopped on the call with Sonia. A few minutes in, I asked, "How is Mark going to handle all these changes that I'm making?" What she said shifted something in me. "You need to keep moving forward and let Mark worry about himself. You don't need his permission and you don't need him to understand. He may never understand, but you need to quit focusing on him and start doing your thing. You need to stop blaming him." I had been blind to the fact that I had been subconsciously using Mark as an excuse and the reason I couldn't move forward. The result of this was an underlying resentment based on the misbelief that he was holding me back, when in fact I was holding myself back. I was afraid he might not approve and that I was letting him down. I felt responsible for his happiness and was stifling my own growth because I intuitively knew it would threaten him and our relationship. *How would my changing impact our marriage?* I also knew Sonia was right. With my newfound awareness, I had no choice. I had to continue on my path, even without knowing what it would mean for our relationship. I was facing a dark cave of uncertainty and needed to find the courage to enter with no guarantee of what the outcome might be.

From that moment on, everything changed. As my feelings began to shift, I realized Mark and I were meant to redefine our relationship. I had been blaming Mark, often subconsciously, for me having given away all my power. It was a turning point for both of us. I was releasing the role of secondary partner and was establishing myself as the co-creating spouse where we stood side by side—as true equals—to create a life together. It was the shift from blaming Mark for the fact that I had taken a secondary role and deciding I needed to take charge of my own life. It was an immediate and instant release of victimhood into a sense of freedom. I was not responsible for Mark's happiness and he was not responsible for mine.

I have witnessed this immediate release in many women who begin to see how they're stuck in the mindset: *If they'll be different then I'll be happy.* When these women shift their belief and begin to take ownership for their own lives and happiness, regardless of the outcome, their anger and resentment just disappears. I've also observed how this blaming and focusing on what the other person needs to do for us to be happy has resulted in a number of relationship breakups. One of my clients said, "Maybe if I had done my own work and changed what I needed to within myself, my marriage would have survived. I always assumed he was the problem, and yet I can now see how I could have been different. At the end of the day, it may not have worked out, but I will always wonder."

The spontaneous and instant release of anger, resentment, and blame happens in those situations when we have a dramatic shift in our beliefs. We begin to see the situation from a completely different perspective. There are many times, however, when transforming anger and resentment is a process requiring time rather than something that happens spontaneously. Those are the times when forgiveness is being called for, in situations when we feel that someone has harmed or hurt us in some way. Times when we notice we're holding onto anger, resentment, and bitterness, and we're carrying a grudge. For many of us on the spiritual path, the process of this forgiveness is an opportunity to grow, evolve, and cultivate compassion.

The Process of Forgiveness

Perhaps one of the most beautiful gifts of feeling anger, resentment, and disappointment is the opportunity it creates for us to learn how to forgive. Life gives us many opportunities to ask ourselves, *Who do I choose to be in this situation and in my life? Do I choose to be hardened and angry with a closed-off heart, or do I choose to be compassionate and loving?* We can either walk around as resentful victims or we can cultivate grace as we embrace forgiveness as a spiritual practice that results in greater love and compassion.

There are significant misunderstandings and confusion about what it means to forgive. Forgiveness enables us to release hurt from the past and transform difficult emotions in the present. It involves our own inner work and the transformation of toxic emotions that we carry around in relation to both others and ourselves. It doesn't mean others are not held accountable for their behavior. It means we take responsibility for releasing the effect these experiences have on our physical and emotional well-being. We make forgiveness about our own peace of mind and not the other person.

The first and probably the most important step in forgiving others is to make the choice—to decide we are ready to let go of holding onto the toxic feelings that arise when we feel someone has wronged us. When we choose to do this, we take a giant step to reclaiming our lives and releasing the energy around anger, resentment, and bitterness. I say choose, because that's what forgiveness is—a choice. Women who remain in a state of anger and resentment are either not ready to make the choice or aren't aware they have one to make.

When we choose to forgive, it's important to understand that forgiveness is a process that takes time. It often requires that we reaffirm our intention on a continual and regular basis. We are also not saying that what happened or the way that we were treated was acceptable. Rather we are saying that we are ready to release the toxic hold that the anger and resentment have on us. While the process of forgiveness often involves a number of steps that are by no means linear, it always begins with the intention or desire to forgive.

I have read a number of books about forgiveness, and I have engaged in many practices. There are processes that include any number of steps, ranging from just a few all the way up to twenty. Twenty steps seemed overwhelming to me, so I decided to condense everything I've read and practiced into six steps. I used the fourfold path described in *The Book of Forgiving* written by Archbishop Desmond Tutu and his daughter, MPHO Tutu, as the foundation. I modified their process to meet my own needs and to blend together a human and spiritual perspective on forgiveness. The four steps I built upon and adapted from the Archbishop's book were: **tell your story; name your hurt; grant forgiveness; and renew or release the relationship**. The Tutus' book includes many beautiful and powerful rituals and practices that support the process of forgiveness, but the idea that we "grant forgiveness" didn't resonate with my own spiritual views, so I modified them and came up with the following six steps:

1. Share your story.

    It's important to openly and honestly share your unedited story with someone you trust. If you don't feel you can do that with another person, it is also effective to write it in your journal or a notebook that you can subsequently destroy or use in the creation of a releasing ritual.

2. Be mindful of your feelings.

    Allowing yourself to feel what you feel is important for transforming your feelings of anger and resentment. We apply the practice of mindfulness that we explored earlier to our feelings, meaning that we become aware of our feelings and create space for them without judgment or denial.

3. Develop a 360-degree perspective.

   During this part of the process we get curious about the other person's perspective and what their story is. We begin to cultivate empathy as we expand our view of the situation and can see that this other person, like us, is human, imperfect, and may have acted out of hurt or pain in their own life.

4. Shift from victim consciousness to seeing the divine plan.

   From a spiritual perspective, we realize that every experience in our life has been created as an opportunity for us to fulfill our Soul's purpose and for growth. From this perspective, people didn't do things *to us*, these situations and people happened *for us*.

5. Create a new relationship or release it all together.

   Every relationship and/or person comes into our life for a reason. There are times we are meant to change ourselves in the relationship and there are other times we're meant to go our separate ways.

6. Forgiveness practice.

   Forgiveness and the transformation of feelings is a process that involves both an intellectual as well as an energetic shift. Spending time in a formal meditation practice focused on forgiveness, creates an opportunity for us to heal at a deeper level that includes the body, mind, and Soul.

This process recognizes the fact that while we are spiritual beings, we are also human beings. It provides a structure and process for forgiveness that begins with telling our story and feeling the hurt and pain that the person or situation triggered in us. If we jump too quickly to developing a broader 360-degree perspective before we've told our story or felt our feelings, we run the risk of not fully forgiving. When we bypass the story and emotions, there's a big risk of denying and turning away from how we're feeling because it feels so uncomfortable. If we jump to forgiveness without first feeling the hurt and telling our story, we are bypassing a vital step in the process and we will stay stuck in the hurt. We don't transform hurt by turning our back on it; we transform it by being with it and allowing ourselves to feel it fully.

Perhaps one of the most profound expressions of forgiveness happens when women develop awareness that to free our Souls and the things that are weighing us down, we need to forgive others—including our parents. I'm always grateful when I have an opportunity to work with women in their twenties and thirties who are willing to transform and release these toxic feelings before they fester for years. The wisdom that is gained through this healing work is beautiful to witness and be a part of.

Forgiving Others, Including Your Parents

Many of us go through adulthood with anger and resentment stemming from childhood. This buildup of toxic emotions often spills over into our adult life and results in physical and emotional health issues. These feelings are firmly planted within us, causing our hearts to remain closed and casting a long shadow on many aspects of our lives.

I met Loraine when we were taking a series of mindfulness classes together, and as we talked about forgiveness, she shared her powerful story with me. Loraine had grown up in a home with an alcoholic mother who she described as "critical, demeaning, selfish, sarcastic and unloving." Although Loraine knew her mother loved her, she never felt loved. Her father had left when she was three years old, and while her mother provided for all her basic needs, she didn't know how to show Loraine and her brother that she loved them. As Loraine sat across from me with tears welling up in her eyes, she shared how she felt "unlovable, unworthy, invisible and like I didn't matter."

As Loraine's mother aged, she began to need a lot of help to deal with her increasing physical frailties. Loraine's brother was not in the picture, and so looking after her aging mother's needs became Loraine's responsibility. This is when she realized she was overflowing with anger and resentment. Here she was, looking after a mother who had never been there for her, while her brother had washed his hands of the entire situation and left the sole responsibility to Loraine.

One day over coffee with a friend, she shared how she was struggling with her feelings towards her mother. Her friend scared her by saying, "If you don't make peace with your mother, she will continue to haunt this life, and your next one and the one after that. She will continue to haunt you until you learn what you're meant to learn from this." This was a terrifying thought for Loraine. "The thought of her continuing to haunt me is unbearable."

Shortly after the lunch with her friend, Loraine attended a service at a local Centre For Spiritual Living. It happened to be Mother's Day and as the minister began to speak, she warned that she was going to share a perspective that might be challenging for some people to hear. She explained that in some metaphysical teachings and cultures, they teach that we choose our parents before we were born. Perhaps there is an intuitive part of us on a Soul level who knows even before we are born who will be our best teachers for a lifetime.

In that moment, something gave way in Loraine and she knew it was the beginning of a shift as she released and transformed the anger, resentment, and bitterness that she held in her heart and the tissues of her body. She began to see how all the experiences she had as a child were part of the plan for her Soul to heal, grow, and evolve. She began to understand her childhood had been a gift that had triggered compassion in her at a young age.

The house of cards that had been built out of resentment and bitterness inside Loraine was starting to crumble. It didn't happen all at once, but it was starting to happen. What had been stuck in her for many years was beginning to loosen, and she knew that to transform it, she needed to take responsibility and stop blaming her mother for how she was feeling.

One of Loraine's favorite forgiveness practices is described in a book called *Zero Limits: The Secret Hawaiian System for Wealth, Health, Peace and More,* which was co-authored by psychiatrist Dr. Hew Len and Joe Vitale. It is an ancient Hawaiian forgiveness practice called Ho'oponopono. It consists of four simple phrases "I love you, I'm sorry, please forgive me, thank you."

As the authors explain:

> "Ho'oponopono is really very simple. For the ancient Hawaiians, all problems begin as thought. But having a thought is not the problem. So what's the problem? The problem is that all our thoughts are imbued with painful memories— memories of persons, places or things. The intellect working alone can't solve

these problems, because the intellect only manages. Managing things is no way to solve problems. You want to let them go! When you do Ho'oponopono, what happens is that the Divinity takes the painful thought and neutralizes or purifies it. You don't purify the person, place, or thing. You neutralize the energy you associate with that person, place, or thing" (2007, pp. 33-34).

Loraine described how on a regular basis she would sit down, close her eyes and repeat the four phrases that made up the practice: *I love you, I'm sorry, please forgive me, thank you.* Using this practice after having worked through the previous steps, she began to notice the ice around her heart was melting. She could feel the shift in herself as she released the resentment that had been building over the years. She was transforming the toxic energy she had felt towards her mother and was releasing the disappointment and guilt she held towards herself. She didn't fully understand how these practices worked…she just knew that they did.

This practice is deeply spiritual in its underlying premise that situations and people are present in our lives in order to heal something within us. It stems from the belief that we are all connected by one conscious mind and that when something is triggered in us, it means something within us needs to be healed. This forgiveness practice reminds us we are not victims of our lives and how people treat us. Rather, we co-create our lives and by changing ourselves, we create a ripple of healing in the world. It is a powerful practice to shift us out of victim consciousness and into accepting responsibility for our lives.

When Loraine got the call that her mom was dying, she knew something in her heart had changed. The message she received at the church that day, combined with the forgiveness meditation she was doing, had shifted things in her.

As she sat with her mother in the final hours, the spiritual advisor from the hospice stopped in to see how she was doing. The advisor could sense the shift in Loraine and said to her, "You've forgiven her, haven't you?" And Loraine knew in that moment that she had. She didn't know exactly when she had released her anger and resentment, she just knew that she had.

Within an hour, her mother had passed away. Loraine said, "Maybe my mom hung on for so long and wasn't ready to go until I had forgiven her. It's like she knew it was okay to go." And then Loraine thought, "Maybe that was a gift that she gave to me so that I wouldn't have to go through the rest of my life feeling this anger and resentment towards her."

As Loraine and I both learned, releasing anger and resentment is not an easy process. It requires the courage to look deeply within ourselves. On our journey towards forgiveness, we are being guided by our Souls, which are always urging and supporting us as we heal and return to wholeness. Perhaps the most valuable and life transforming practice to ease the suffering that is a close and constant companion on our journey towards awakening, is self-compassion. On my own journey, I was about to learn that being compassionate with others doesn't always equate with being compassionate with ourselves. This realization was about to shift my entire way of being in every aspect of my life.

Awakening Your Soul

Misbelief: When others change, you'll feel happier and more peaceful.
Truth: You need to change yourself in the relationship and establish a new way of being in order to change patterns and ways of being that aren't an expression of your Soul.

Misbelief: Forgiveness means that what happened was okay.
Truth: The anger, resentment, bitterness, disappointment, shame, and hurt that we are transforming is for our own inner peace and has nothing to do with the other person.

Misbelief: Feeling anger and resentment doesn't feel good, but it's justified.
Truth: These feelings of constriction will become toxic in our body, causing physical and emotional health issues. There are practices and processes that will help transform this energy to a higher vibrational emotion.

Practices/Reflections

1. Begin to notice when you blame others for the way you're feeling. Whether it's when someone pushes your buttons or an entire relationship that has been challenging for you. Ask yourself, *Am I willing to transform these feelings and change something within myself?*

2. Pick one person/situation that you would say is a strained (not traumatic) relationship. Work through the 6-step process outlined in this chapter.

3. Spend a few minutes every day doing a forgiveness meditation. It may be the Ho'oponopono practice outlined in this chapter or another one you find.

CHAPTER 6

Self-Compassion is Non-Negotiable

"Maybe what people need to make meaningful change is feeling like they are already worthy, already accepted and already loved for exactly who they are."

— *Susan*

When I was a young girl my dad was transferred a lot for work, so my sisters and I got used to making new friends. I was seven years old when we moved to a small town in Ontario. One of my dad's favorite sayings when we moved to a new place was "go out and play...make friends."

One fall day as the leaves were turning the most amazing colors, my sister Nora and I went out to play and met some girls that lived a couple of houses down. Before long, Nora and I found ourselves in a fun game of tag as we chased each other around the neighborhood laughing and squealing. I was a shy and quiet girl and so I felt pretty good about having these new girls to play with. I didn't realize it at the time that one of the sisters we were playing with had a reputation of being the neighborhood bully. Without me seeing it coming, the bully wound up and hit me in the head with a stick that happened to have a nail in it. She had thought I was getting a little too close to her older sister and decided to put an end to our little game of tag. That incident was about to change the course of my life.

With blood trickling down my face, Nora rushed me home to our parents who brought me to the hospital for stitches. I sat in the emergency room, on a cold stretcher, alone and terrified, with a cloth over my head that left me in total darkness. Then the hand of a nurse gently embraced my own. The love, compassion, kindness, and sheer presence in that simple gesture left an impression on me that shaped my entire life. She offered a few soft words, telling me, "You're going to be okay and I will stay with you the whole time. You don't need to be afraid."

Her words and loving presence enabled me to get through that experience because I knew I wasn't alone. Those words were also the reason I became a nurse, devoting thirty years to a calling that gave me the privilege of being with people who were at vulnerable places in their lives, much the way I had been as a little girl. I sat with people who were dying, comforted people who were watching people they love slip away due to Alzheimer's disease, and heard about near-death experiences that left people believing there is more to this life than what we can see. I felt such a deep sense of love for and connection with so many of the people that I met on my path.

I witnessed first-hand the transformative power of compassion. I always believed my role as a nurse was to be a "nurturing gardener, not a fix-it mechanic." As a palliative care nurse, I saw a great deal of suffering. I helped alleviate physical discomfort to the best of my ability, and I tried to be a compassionate presence. Just as that nurse was for me when I was a little girl, I wanted to be there for other people in way that was loving, kind, and left them knowing they weren't alone.

In the presence of compassion, love, and acceptance, people were free to share their deepest truths and their greatest fears. Decades later as my mind began to settle, I could sense that my Soul was aching for this same compassion that I had received from a stranger, so many years ago.

As often happens when we become open and aware enough, we receive messages from the universe guiding us toward our next step. The message I received was on a Saturday morning in an email about an upcoming workshop in Calgary about "Mindful Self-Compassion" based on the work of Dr. Kristin Neff Ph.D, an associate professor at the University of Austin, Texas. I had just started teaching meditation and mindfulness and was curious about this concept of self-compassion. My mindfulness practice was making it really apparent to me that I could be pretty hard on myself. I also noticed the same thing in the women I was teaching. They'd say things like: "I find it easier to be kind to others but not myself." "I learned I was supposed to just suck it up when I was having a hard time." "I was taught that only certain feelings are okay." "I can be hard on myself when I feel I've failed at something." I didn't realize this workshop was about to change my relationship with my Self.

Attending the workshop made me realize that I hadn't been there for myself in the same way that I had been there for other people who were suffering. I began to explore what self-compassion might look and feel like if I cultivated it within myself. I came to learn that the practice of self-compassion is an act of self-soothing, and I was reminded how natural it is to self-soothe by my little grandson, Johnny. Whenever I spent time with him, I would notice how his thumb would make its way to his mouth when he was tired, so that he could comfort himself and fall asleep. Or how, when he woke in the middle of the night crying, he would use his thumb to sooth himself back to sleep. This self-soothing skill that babies have is something that we lose along the way as we become adults.

Dr. Neff's pioneering research and work on self-compassion has made a dramatic impact on the awareness and ability of many of us to self-soothe and to cultivate self-compassion and kindness towards ourselves. Her book *Self-Compassion: The Proven Power of Being Kind to Yourself* provides a simple and easy, step-by-step process to teach us how to be kinder with ourselves when we're feeling stressed by both the big and little things in our lives.

Self-compassion helps us deal with situations that range from someone cutting in front of us in the grocery store lineup, to sitting in the doctor's office waiting to hear if a biopsy is positive for cancer. It is powerful and practical because it doesn't require us to sit down to meditate or allocate a certain amount of time to practice. All it requires is the awareness of how to do it—and then remembering to use it when we notice we are having a hard time. It gives our mind a way to deal with the struggles in life that is healthy, comforting, compassionate, and transformative.

When I arrived home from the workshop, I sat down for a few minutes and completed the self-compassion quiz that you'll find on the Self-Compassion website (http://self-compassion.org). Completing this quiz was quite a rude awakening for me. I realized I had spent my whole life valuing compassion, but never directing it towards myself. By the time I finished the short quiz, I knew I was on the road to developing a new relationship with my mind and my Self. Now that I knew what it meant to be more self-compassionate, inner peace would elude me if I didn't develop this skill.

Dr. Neff explains that self-compassion encompasses three main components which, when practiced in our life, create a new way of being for many of us. A way of being that allows us to deal with whatever life throws at us from a place of compassion and acceptance, rather than expectations of perfection. The three components are **mindfulness vs. over-identification, common humanity, and self-kindness vs. self-judgment**.

Mindfulness vs. over-identification involves being with our thoughts and feelings in moments when we're suffering in a way that creates space for them to exist, without denying or exaggerating them. *Common humanity* reminds us that every human being has moments of suffering and that we are not alone. This sense of not feeling isolated in our difficult times or moments provide a sense of comfort. *Self-kindness vs. self-judgment* enables us to embrace the idea that we're not perfect. We develop the ability to be kind to ourselves—without being judgmental or self-critical—during the times we feel inadequate or are suffering.

Before going on, pause for a moment and ask yourself the following questions: *How do I talk to myself when I'm feeling stressed, frustrated, sad, impatient, embarrassed, ashamed, lonely, angry, restless, or any other number of emotions that feel uncomfortable? Do I try to talk myself out of my feelings, telling myself that many others have it a lot worse than I do? Do I try to distract myself or turn away from my feelings by going to the fridge for some cake or another glass of wine, or going on a shopping spree? Do I tell myself I really shouldn't feel the way that I do? Do I feel isolated when I'm having a hard time? Is that little voice inside my head talking to me like my best friend would, or is it like a bad roommate?*

Self-compassion is about learning to be our own best friend when we're having a hard time. A best friend who tells you that they get it because they've been there, too—and that you're not alone. A friend who creates space for you to feel your feelings without judgment or telling you it's wrong to feel the way you do. Someone who knows that if you resist what you're feeling, it persists and shows up as physical or emotional issues. A friend who knows exactly what you need to hear in that moment. She knows when you need a hug, a cup of tea, or a walk outside. She doesn't feed into a pity party; rather, she journeys with you as she expresses unconditional love and acceptance.

Self-Compassion in Action

The universe, which always gives us what we need and not what we want, was about to give me an opportunity to practice my newfound skill of being more self-compassionate. Several months after I completed the self-compassion workshop, I began to have some strange physical symptoms and knew there was something wrong with me. I was having difficulty sleeping at night because I felt so revved up. I could feel my heart pounding out of my chest at times, had fuzzy thinking, and was losing weight without trying or doing anything different. While I was glad my jeans were fitting well, I knew something was off. After several doctor's visits and blood tests, they decided I had something wrong with my thyroid. To ensure it wasn't something more serious, they did a biopsy.

As I sat in the doctor's office waiting for the results, I knew it was the perfect opportunity to practice self-compassion. My appointment was at 10 a.m. and at 10:45, I was still sitting there. I was already a bit nervous about the results, and the added time was really building my anxiety. In the past, not knowing what to do with the fact that I was feeling anxious, I would have told myself things such as: *You're being ridiculous because compared to what most people go through, this is nothing. You really shouldn't be feeling this way. I wish I would stop feeling so anxious. Why is she (the doctor) always late? This waiting is driving me crazy. What happens if I have cancer? Suck it up and quit being such a baby.*

The untrained mind can be quite unruly and, left to its own devices, it doesn't know how to respond to these difficult moments in a kind and nourishing way. In the process of trying to get away from the uncomfortable feelings, we actually make them worse and we end up feeling more of what we don't want, which is discomfort.

Armed with the self-compassion formula and an awareness of the three components, I responded to my discomfort in the doctor's office this way: first, I noticed my anxiety and instead of beating myself up about it, I began to gently rub my arm and reassure myself with a loving touch while telling myself *"I am okay"* (mindfulness vs. over- identification). As Dr. Neff explains, this physical touch releases oxytocin, also known as the cuddle hormone, and is released when we are hugging or breastfeeding newborns. It's the hormone of love and connection and provides a sense of comfort.

As a second step in this mindfulness process, I labeled what I was feeling—*this is a moment of suffering and I'm feeling really anxious*—and allowed it to be there without trying to deny it or talk myself out of it. I became curious about how this anxiety felt in my body. *How long did it last? How intense was it? Where did I feel it?* Allowing ourselves to feel what we feel is critical, as our natural tendency is to turn away from uncomfortable feelings and try to get rid of them.

Next, I told myself that *suffering is part of life and that I'm not alone* (common humanity). We all have times in our lives when we're suffering or having a hard time. This step really calmed me down. I was surprised how it shifted something in me as I had a sense that others have also experienced this. It left me feeling connected to others rather than isolated; the way we commonly feel when we think we're the only one who ever experiences these things.

Finally, I asked myself what I needed in that moment and how I could be kind to myself (self-kindness vs. self-judgment). I told myself that *no matter what, I'm going to be okay. I am safe. Feeling anxious is normal. Just focus on my breath and take some long, slow, deep breaths.* It is in this final step that we draw on our inner wisdom as we ask ourselves to be there for ourselves as if we are a good friend. We are kind, compassionate, and loving of what we are experiencing in the moment.

Being self-compassionate is valuable both in our day-to-day life as well as in our journey towards awakening our Souls. The process of transformation and change is often uncertain and sometimes challenging as we're emerging into a new way of being. We're dealing with feelings we've previously tucked away, and we're transforming anger and resentment as we move towards forgiveness. We've begun to see how we may have let ourselves or other people down. Shifting from our Small Self to our Soul requires courage and often feels uncomfortable. Having the ability to be self-compassionate during the process is a gift. The other truth about transformation is that the majority of us who are drawn to do this inner work, are often brought to it as a result of some degree of suffering. We usually don't make the changes when things are going great.

The Purpose of Suffering

For two years following my return to Calgary, Mark and I would spend months away from each other as I was in Calgary and he'd continue to go to Phoenix for six months at a time. During that time, I experienced an inner ache and longing that became my close and constant companion. I found myself asking: *What is the purpose of all of this? Why do I need to make these changes? Is my marriage going to survive this? Am I going to survive this?* I was suffering and spent a great deal of energy resisting what was going on in my life. I didn't like uncertainty and I was used to being in control. This resistance just seemed to add to my suffering and yet I didn't know any other way. One night as I lay in bed alone, deeply missing Mark, I closed my eyes and began to pray. *I really don't understand what is happening to me or why I'm going through this. I'm done trying to figure it out and I surrender. If there's something out there that's bigger than me, I need you.*

I had never prayed before in my life. I really didn't know what prayer was because I had never gone to church or been exposed to it as a child. But now, without yet realizing it, I had let my Small Self step aside and allowed my Soul to move into the driver's seat. That small moment of turning my worry into a prayer that came from some place deep inside me was the beginning of a new relationship with an intelligent life force larger than myself.

On a Sunday morning several weeks later, I found myself attending The Calgary Centre For Spiritual Living. As the singing began, emotion welled up in my throat. My eyes became watery and I knew that I had been led to this place for a reason. The minister talked about one power that flows through us and around us. She talked about the fact there are as many paths to this life force as there are people on this planet and that this intelligence is not separate from us, rather we are an expression of this one life force. While our life circumstances may not always reflect it, at our core we are pure love. Her message that day felt as if it had been written specifically for me and answered what all my suffering was about. The minister said that this higher intelligence that needs to be expressed through us is always growing and evolving. This process of becoming a spiritual being having a human experience can be difficult as we're called to shed what no longer serves us.

The message that became crystal clear to me that day was that the suffering was about letting go of the old in order to embrace my Soul. It was my Small Self that was putting up the fuss and not wanting me to change, while my Soul, which aligned with an intelligent life force, was creating space for me to shift my life. In this moment, I knew my suffering was there for a reason and the more I resisted, the greater the suffering would be.

The Buddhist proverb "pain is inevitable; suffering is optional" began to make sense to me. None of us get through life without having painful things happen to us. When we resist the flow of nature and what is happening, the pain turns into suffering. The pain in our lives is our trigger for growth and awakening. When we come at these experiences from the perspective of self-compassion, our pain doesn't need to turn into suffering. Instead, we allow ourselves to simply *be* with the experiences and to understand the deeper meaning.

Just as I began to understand the difference between the pain and suffering in my own life, I had another shift in my views—this time about my role as a parent. Ultimately, the pain that had happened in life was leading me down a path towards greater inner peace and alignment with my Soul. If this was true for me, wasn't it also true for our children and others we care about when they're going through hard times? I had always believed my role was to make my kids and others happy and shelter them from pain. Thich Nhat Hanh's quote "no mud, no lotus" reminds us that this is neither possible nor desirable. In his book, *No Mud, No Lotus: The Art of Transforming Suffering,* he identifies that: "Without suffering, there's no happiness. So we shouldn't discriminate against the mud to help the flower of happiness grow. There can be no lotus flower without the mud" (2014, p.13). I was beginning to see that perhaps there was greater wisdom in teaching our children how to be with pain in a way that doesn't lead to greater suffering, as opposed to believing we are meant to prevent them from ever having pain in the first place.

In response to those times in our lives when we feel we are suffering, we have two choices. Either we can be compassionate and kind with ourselves or we can be hard and critical of ourselves. Responding to our suffering and the suffering of others with compassion rather than judgment, creates space for a transformation to occur. As we respond to our own suffering with compassion, we develop a new relationship with our Self and our suffering lessens. The ability to be with our suffering eases the resistance to the suffering that we witness in others. Watching people we love experience pain in their lives is one of the hardest things we can go through, but when we know it's all part of the evolution of their Soul, we can journey with them with less resistance and more grace. We are all in this together.

Self-Compassion vs. Self-Care

A lot of women get confused about the difference between self-care and self-compassion. While self-care is important, it is not necessarily the same as self-compassion. It is possible for women to engage in numerous self-care activities and yet still be very hard on themselves. Self-care is often associated with taking care of our physical bodies, but having strong and fit bodies doesn't necessarily mean we won't still feel lost and disconnected from our Souls.

I experienced this firsthand when I was a mom with two young kids at home. I found the adjustment to being a stay-at-home mom stressful. I was used to having lots of freedom and when I found myself exhausted, overwhelmed, and lacking stimulating adult connections, I realized I needed to take better care of myself. So I arranged for some self-care. I'd have a baby sitter or a family member come over for a couple of hours so I could go out and get my nails done, have a massage, get a haircut, or have lunch with a friend. But while I loved every moment of being out, I came home still exhausted. Then I'd feel guilty knowing most people in the world didn't have the luxury of pedicures and massages, and my guilt would leave me feeling even more drained. My idea of self-care was great in theory, but it wasn't penetrating enough to provide the deeper nourishment I needed.

For many women, giving themselves permission to practice the most basic level of self-care can be challenging. Most of us are conditioned to believe our value and worth comes from sacrificing our Self and our needs for others. We are taught to think about others before ourselves, and that the more we give, the more worthy of love we are. These beliefs, which most of us aren't even aware of, leave us feeling as if we don't have the right for even our basic self-care needs to be met.

Self-care is part of basic survival. Without it, there is no way that we will thrive in our lives. As one woman said, "I felt really guilty for wanting to do things to take care of myself. I almost felt like I didn't have the right to ask that of my husband because my job was to look after the kids and his job was to go out and work so that I could have the luxury of staying home. This luxury of staying home actually started to feel more like a prison to me. I had lost my freedom."

The Mindful Self-Compassion workshop I referred to earlier shared another practice that I thought was helpful. The presenter spoke about the tendency of women to give and give and give and give, until we *gasp* to catch our breath. The workshop facilitator explained that instead of giving until we literally can't breathe, we need to remind ourselves that the natural flow of our breath is *in, out, in, out*—and so on. When we create a way of being that creates space for taking in air and nourishment in equal balance with what we give out, we can give infinitely. The problem with women is not that we give too much, but that we don't give proportionately to ourselves.

Self-Love

If self-care involves those things that we do to care for ourselves, and self-compassion is how we treat ourselves when we're suffering, what is self-love? Self-love is the ultimate part of our inner Self and it permeates everything in our lives. When we have self-love, we have self-compassion and we embrace self-care. It is an agreement that we make with ourselves to love our Self unconditionally, no matter what. When we love our Self, no matter what, we are able to love others, no matter what. When we don't love our Self, we aren't able to feel the love from other people, no matter how much they care for us. Learning how to love, accept, honor, and make space for all the fragmented imperfections that make up our being, is ultimately what our life is all about.

I loved how a client of mine described it: "Self-love was about bringing light to my dark areas. As long as I left those parts in the dark, they remained dark. Like my worries about being a perfectionist, or that I may fail or not be accepted. So I acknowledged and brought light to them by also loving those parts of myself. When I do this, they don't weigh me down anymore. They just seem to dissolve."

Self-love is the language of our Souls. It is the Soul saying: *I love you no matter what. You are good enough and you are meant to embrace all of your imperfections.* As the voice of our Soul gets louder, it begins to drown out the Small Self's voice that says: *If I show you the real me, you won't love, like, or accept me. You need to change because who you are isn't good enough.*

It is our Small Self that has us walking around with masks on. We live in a constant paradox. On one hand, it is our deepest desire to fully express who we are at our core and be loved by others for it. On the other hand, we are afraid to show up without our masks because we fear that if our true selves are exposed, we won't be good enough. One woman put it this way, "One of my biggest fears is being seen as not having it all together. So, I went around hiding my true Self and felt like a fake or fraud. At any moment, someone would find out about the real me and so it was safer to hide behind the smoke screen." She went on to say "Nobody wants to see a broken Soul."

This misbelief that leads us to hide behind our masks is like a self-fulfilling prophecy. Our fear of showing our true Self because we think we won't be loved, is what ultimately prevents us from connecting with others in ways that enable us to give and receive the love and connection we desire. John Powell, a Jesuit priest, wrote a little book called, *Why Am I Afraid to Tell You Who I Am?* Powell shared how one respondent answered the question, which was at the root of our fear: "But, if I tell you who I am, you may not like who I am, and it is all that I have" (1969, p. 4). He goes on to say that to be happy, grow, and really come alive, we need to be able to share our deepest truths with another person. But what does he mean by our deepest truths?

As Powell explains, "I have to be free and able to say my thoughts to you, to tell you about my judgments and values, to expose to you my fears and frustrations, to admit to you my failures and shames, to share my triumphs, before I can really be sure what it is that I am and can become. I must be able to tell you who I am before I can know who I am. And I must know who I am before I can act truly, that is, in accordance with my true self" (p. 25).

As long as we believe we won't be loved for who we are, imperfections and all, we won't fully become ourselves. We need to risk vulnerability and to believe in our self-worth and value it enough to at times ruffle some feathers. We need to fully open ourselves up in relationship with other people if we are committed to awakening our Souls. It is through communication with others that we awaken and become fully ourselves.

But instead, many women say, feel, and act the way we believe we *should* in order to be accepted and fit in. We hide behind our roles and put all our energy into winning the best supporting actress role by being the best wife, mother, friend, parent, daughter, and so on. And in the process of attempting to be all things to all people, we lose ourselves.

My Soul recognized that I had lost myself as a result of the many years of trying to be all things to all people and it was carrying out a revolt. After reading John Powell's book, I was able to see that I had lost myself, but I had no idea *why* I had lost myself. By this point in my transformation, I had settled my mind and nervous system, became more aware and accepting of my thoughts and feelings, and I had made progress in releasing anger and resentment. But while I had made significant changes, I still hadn't fully transformed my way of being. I was hungry for self-love.

Cultivating self-love for our personality quirks and embracing ourselves for exactly who we are is what self-love is all about. One of my clients put it this way, "This is me and this is who I am. You either like me or you don't and I'm okay with that." I loved Brené Brown's definition of self-love in her book, *The Gifts of Imperfection: Let Go of Who You Think You're Supposed to Be and Embrace Who You Are.* She explained that "practicing self-love means learning how to trust ourselves, to treat ourselves with respect, and to be kind and affectionate towards ourselves" (2010, p. 27). Imagine the inner power that we feel when we embrace ourselves exactly as we are. No more masks, hiding, or letting our Small Self rule our lives with fear.

There's a practice I have found powerful for working with the tendency of our minds to be harsh and critical with ourselves. Let's use being judgmental as an example. We know how destructive being judgmental can be in both our relationships and how we feel about ourselves. For many of us, being judgmental is an ingrained habit. When we notice we're thinking judgmental thoughts, our natural response is to say: *I shouldn't feel this way. What a loser I am. Why am I so judgmental?* By talking to ourselves in this way, we're actually turning a natural human tendency and the fact we're not perfect into a moment of shame.

Coming at this from the perspective of self-love looks and feels very different. Instead of beating ourselves up for having judgmental thoughts, we say instead, *Even though I am being judgmental, I completely accept and love myself.* It's a powerful shift because we are cultivating the ability to notice our thoughts and be mindful, accepting what is, and at the same time, loving ourselves unconditionally. We don't just love ourselves when we're being perfect, we love ourselves no matter what.

A client of mine began asking herself, "If I'm not full of self-love, what am I full of?" That's a great question. As her awareness increased, this client began to notice her mind was full of all sorts of thoughts and stories that were filling up the space meant for self-love and acceptance. By increasing our loving awareness of our judgmental thoughts, we can choose to replace them with more nourishing thoughts that enhance the relationship both with ourselves and with others.

Developing self-love for ourselves means we need to love it all, including our bodies. I have noticed most women have some sort of hate on for some part of their body. It may be for having excessive weight, poor skin, too may wrinkles, too much cellulite, or less than perky boobs. For others who have an illness of some sort, it may be a disappointment or anger for how an organ has let them down or how an unwelcome disease such as cancer has entered their body.

Loving ourselves, including all of our physical imperfections, is a practice most of us need to cultivate. It's virtually impossible to awaken your Soul when you can't stand some part of yourself. Shifting from the *I'll feel good about myself when I've lost weight or when this disease goes away* to *I love all the parts of myself including my physical imperfections,* is when healing begins. The common saying that "what we resist, persists" also goes for the physical stuff in our body.

Most mornings during my meditation when I'm doing a body scan, I send loving attention and messages to all parts of my body, especially those parts I used to look at in disgust. I send deep gratitude and love to it all, and through this practice I feel I have shifted to a place of self-acceptance and love. I send love to my thyroid that has been under functioning and visualize that, through my loving awareness, it is healing and functioning again. I don't know precisely what caused the changes, but my need for thyroid boosting has substantially lessened. With the introduction of meditation and mindfulness, I have created an environment for healing in my body.

I recently watched the 2017 documentary *HEAL,* featuring luminaries in the field of healing, science, and transformation. It's a documentary that takes us on a spiritual and scientific journey to understand how our thoughts, beliefs, and emotions have an impact on our health and ability to heal. I was reminded of the power of the body to heal itself when we create an environment of self-love. From a spiritual and scientific perspective, the documentary explores how we are not victims of our genes and how we have more control over our health and life than we were taught to believe. ***Awakening a Woman's Soul*** is about healing and transformation at the deepest levels. Every part of us, including our cells, needs a loving environment to thrive. When we practice unconditional self-love with ourselves, we begin to heal on a physical, emotional, and spiritual level.

One of the most powerful shifts that occurred as a result of my mindfulness and self-compassion practice was the ability to cultivate self-love and acceptance. As I became aware of my thoughts, I began to notice how often I had that little voice in my head telling me I wasn't good enough or smart enough, along with many other comments that left me feeling utterly unloved. When I began to notice how I was speaking to myself and embraced that little voice without going to battle with it, I began to cultivate self-love.

I realize now that it was a lack of self-love being expressed when I was so resistant to meditation in the first place. Underneath all my excuses for why I thought meditation wasn't for me, lay the fear of spending five minutes alone with my thoughts and myself.

Growing and evolving in self-love is the fertilizer for creating an inner environment where our Souls can begin to speak and become fully expressed in all aspects of our lives. When we love ourselves unconditionally, we become unstoppable. We start caring as much about ourselves as we do others. We let our creative energy flow out into the world; knowing that no matter what, we are loved. We express ourselves fully in our relationships because we know that we can and will still love ourselves unconditionally, even if (and when) we don't always say the right things.

Every moment and aspect of this dance towards connecting and allowing our Soul to be expressed through us is ultimately about self-love. Every step we take towards becoming more self-loving is a step towards inner peace and fulfillment. It means we will attract a loving relationship, find work that is meaningful, have deep friendships, make a difference in the world, and be lit with an inner sparkle.

Awakening Your Soul

Misbelief: You are more worthy and lovable if you are selfless and sacrifice yourself to give to others.
Truth: You are worthy and are meant to love yourself for exactly who you are. You don't need to do or be different in order to love yourself or to be lovable.

Misbelief: Being self-compassionate will make you weaker and less motivated to be successful.
Truth: Being self-compassionate will create a new way of being that enables you to flourish in all areas of your life.

Misbelief: Self-care and self-love are the same thing.
Truth: Self-care is about what you do, and self-love is about who you are. You are meant to love yourself unconditionally and that means your imperfections as well.

Practices/Reflections

1. Learn more and complete the self-compassion quiz developed by Dr. Kristin Neff at http://self-compassion.org/test-how-self-compassionate-you-are/. What did you learn about yourself from completing the quiz?

2. Practice the five-minute Self-Compassion Break when you're suffering, feeling inadequate, or having a hard time: http://selfcompassion.org/category/exercises/.

3. Begin to notice and write in your journal about situations and times when you feel you're "not enough." Start each day by looking in the mirror and saying, "I love you, _____." Notice if you experience any resistance in your body when practicing this.

CHAPTER 7

The Art of Hearing Your Soul

The real voyage of discovery consists not in seeking new landscapes,
but in having new eyes.

— *T.S. Eliot*

In the months away from Mark, when I was journeying alone, I began to notice my usual way of being wasn't serving me any longer. I had always been the kind of woman who needed to feel in control of my life and "have it all figured out." I was slowly beginning to realize that coming at life from this perspective wasn't working and was keeping me small and often afraid. My intellect and the thinking mind I had always valued, which had enabled me to excel in school and earn a graduate degree, wasn't able to "figure things out" anymore. My need to figure it out was leading me instead to doing more and searching more—and with a headache. My meditation and mindfulness practice made it painfully obvious that for most of my life I had been living my life primarily in my head with a total disconnect from my Soul, heart, and body. I was bursting to create a new way of being—and it was about to turn my whole life upside down.

In the years after I left my career in nursing, Mark and I went on some amazing adventures. In addition to climbing Mount Kilimanjaro, we cycled in Italy, went ice climbing in New Zealand, visited Alaska, golfed and toured in Asia, trekked the Camino in Spain and hiked into Machu Pichu in Peru. Each of these trips was an adventure of a lifetime and I knew how fortunate I was to experience these amazing places. I had always loved adventure and the trips were part of my need to seek and find some answers in my life. What I was to eventually discover was that the very thing I sought while on all these trips was with me all along: *my Self!*

I realized I had been travelling all over the world to find the answers already inside me. I just hadn't paused long enough to find them—or known how to look. As my mind became settled through meditation and I cleared away the garbage that had accumulated through the caterpillar phase of my life, I was creating space for a new way of being to emerge. A way of being that reflected what my Soul needed to thrive, instead of perpetually feeding the Small Self that left me hungry for more—more drama, more distractions, more things to do, more people to see, more money, more shoes, purses, and more spiritual entertainment.

While the Small Self needs more of the outer stuff in our lives, the Soul needs something very different: silence and space from our busy, hectic, and overly distracted lives. As I gave my Soul the space, I began to hear it speaking to me through my intuition and my inner wisdom— it was guiding me to be different in all parts of my life.

My journey had been like Dorothy's in the movie, *The Wizard of Oz*. Dorothy's journey began when she was swept away from a farm in Kansas by a tornado and landed in the magical land of Oz. Dorothy travelled with her companions—the Scarecrow, Tin Man, and the Cowardly Lion, in search of The Great and Powerful Oz, whom she believed had the power to help her return home to Kansas. After a long journey, however, Dorothy realized that she'd had the power all along and that all she needed to do was tap into it through her beautiful ruby red slippers.

Watching this movie was one of my favorites things to do as a young girl. Once every year, my sisters and I would set up our TV trays and watch *The Wizard of Oz* while we ate supper. Perhaps the movie spoke to my Soul because it was foreshadowing the journey I would embark on later in my own life—a journey to discover that while we're overcoming our fears, finding our courage, and connecting with our hearts, we possess within ourselves the power all the way along. We come to understand that we and we alone take this journey. No one can take it for us as we overcome the obstacles on the road to awakening our Souls.

While I travelled around the world looking for answers I assumed were outside of me, many women are likewise travelling around their cities looking for similar answers. While my seeking brought me to exotic places, others' seeking may bring them to drumming circles, meditations, shamanic rituals, full moon ceremonies, psychic and medium readings, crystal bowl gatherings and countless other spiritual practices aimed at getting people in touch with themselves. With all this searching, at some point your Soul may ask: *Are all of these things that I'm doing bringing me closer to what I'm seeking? And what exactly am I seeking?* The famous Rumi quote, "What you seek is seeking you," reminds us that there is something inside us that needs to be expressed through us. This need for expression is a call from an intelligent life force. It is seeking us because it is attempting to get our attention. Many of us respond to this inner call by looking outside ourselves and trying to figure it out, when in fact, we're being called to go inward and connect with our inner wisdom.

I was at a point in my transformation where I was curious about my intuition and ways of knowing beyond my thinking mind and five senses. I was ready to have those "new eyes" that T.S. Eliot referred to and open to a new perspective: a way of seeing that would equip me to look at the world through the eyes of the Soul and Spirit, rather than from my conditioned and habitual way of thinking. I realized that the belief that the only "real" things in life are those we can experience with our five senses was false, and that there is much more waiting to be uncovered. I was gaining clarity about the fact that more stuff, food, friends, money, trips, or traditional definitions of success weren't going to feed my Soul. I was beginning to get a sense that there was more to life than meets the eye and I wondered: *If we're not our minds then who are we? How do we connect with a life force greater than us? Where do non-physical beings like angels, Spirit guides, deceased loved ones, and other invisible forces fit into our lives? How do we cultivate intuition? Is intuitive even reliable?* When I began asking these questions and was open to receiving the answers, my life got really interesting. It became mystical, and it was the beginning of a complete and total new way of being. I was beginning to see the world and my life with a whole new set of eyes. I realized that I had been living with tunnel vision from my Small

Self and that these questions created space for a complete transformation to a life led by my Soul.

Cultivating Intuition and Inner Wisdom

Our intuition is like an inner navigation system that guides us home to our deepest truths, which are housed in our Souls. Intuition is a way of knowing that extends beyond our five senses. It's a knowing that reveals itself by way of a creative idea or solution, a gut feeling, or a sixth sense about something. It's that sense that we know the answer without knowing how we know. We just know. Intuition is not based on facts, past experiences, or logical thinking. It is an awareness that arises from someplace beyond our thinking mind. It's surprising and yet not surprising that a significant number of people don't trust intuition as a reliable source of information. Although research has long since proven that intuition is a real phenomenon, it continues to play second fiddle to our logical, rational mind—perhaps because we don't understand how it works.

My son Scott taught me a powerful lesson about inner knowing. When Scott was ten years old, his grandpa passed away. The night after he died, Mark, Scott and I were sitting in the hot tub in our backyard looking out at a night sky littered with stars. As we soaked, we began to talk about his grandpa and I said, "I wonder if Grandpa is out there someplace in heaven." Without hesitation, Scott chimed in and with great authority said, "Heaven isn't out there someplace. Heaven is inside of us. When someone we love dies a little bit of them goes into the hearts of everyone that loves them." *How did Scott know this?* He had never been to church and this conversation had never come up. He knew it because there are some things that we just know. We don't know how we know them, we just know.

That is what intuition and inner knowing is all about. Inner wisdom, intuition, guidance, or inner voice are all part of the universe's intelligence. It is how the universe communicates with us and the more we hone the skill and follow its direction, the more we'll thrive physically, emotionally, and spiritually in our lives. It lets us know when we're on the right track and whether the choices we are making are aligned with our highest good or whether they're in service of our Small Self. It's like the sensor on the car that begins beeping when you're getting off track and might hit another car or something else. Our intuition is similar in that it lets us know when we're both on track and getting off track. The trick is to trust and listen to it. Most of us have been conditioned to believe that our thinking mind has all the answers. We ignore or down play the importance and value of our intuition and inner knowing. Albert Einstein reminded us that, "The intuitive mind is a sacred gift and the rational mind is a faithful servant. We have created a society that honors the servant and has forgotten the gift."

Our lives come back into a natural balance when we learn to use our rational mind in service of our Soul as opposed to the other way around.

Intuition and inner wisdom live in the spaces and gaps between our thoughts and are never found in the habitual, often repetitive thinking that goes through our minds.

The voice of inner wisdom is quiet and shy and often gets drowned out by the louder voices both inside of us and around us. We are so accustomed to living our lives with an outward focus, that we have ignored the most valuable and important source of inner wisdom found in the little voice inside of us. Even when we do hear that voice, it's not uncommon to experience resistance to trusting it. We believe others are smarter, wiser, and know what's best for us. We value other opinions over our own and we move through the world feeling disconnected from our inner truths.

I often hear women say that they can hear the voice of their inner wisdom, but they're afraid to act on it. So they shut it down and try and ignore it, convincing themselves that it's likely not the "truth." But what if your inner wisdom is telling you that you're in a relationship that won't enable you to grow? What if it is having you question whether you're in the right job? What if it is telling you that your physical health is suffering because you have some undigested emotional issues? What next? The harsh truth is that we spend a lot of time and energy talking ourselves out of what our inner wisdom is telling us. The universe is relentless however, and you'll keep getting warning signs and messages that will escalate until you listen.

Jessica, a bright and energetic single woman, laughed when she told me, "For the past fourteen years, I had my psychic on speed dial." Every time she met a guy, she explained, "I would run to her to figure out if this was "the one". She'd tell me if it was going to work out and I'd have total trust in what she said."

Jessica went on to say that she had been dating someone off and on for two and a half years. Her psychic told her she had a good feeling about this one and that it was all going to work out, but Jessica had a feeling that things weren't right and that he wasn't the one. This created what she described as "a lot of turmoil and confusion. I wanted to trust her because I wanted the relationship to work out so badly and yet deep down I knew it wasn't going to." But she hung in there, hoping that things would work out.

As Jessica shared her story, her eyes became teary. "It was crazy. Why would I trust someone else over my own inner wisdom and what felt right and good? I guess I just stopped listening and paying attention to what my gut was saying."

Several months later, Jessica decided, "That was it, no more psychics!" When I asked her why she had made this decision, she said, "I started a new job and my supervisor told me that I was too hard on myself and that it was okay if I made mistakes. That statement really hit me hard," she explained, "I started to ask myself what my issue was with not feeling it was okay to make mistakes. I realized that I had been seeing a psychic because I was afraid to make mistakes, and I didn't trust that I could make good decisions. I wanted to have it all figured out and take all the risk out of it."

Jessica realized she had never trusted or valued her inner wisdom and always went to other people, whether it was her mother, a psychic, or supervisor for decisions. When she talked about her inner wisdom, she said, "I didn't even realize it was an option, but now I'm ready to say screw what the rest of the world thinks because it's my life and my decisions."

As Jessica discovered in the process of awakening her Soul, we need to learn to trust our inner voice and not allow our inner knowing to be drowned out by other people's opinions or our Small Self. Jessica spent more than two years trying to talk herself out of what she knew inside was the truth— the relationship was not right for her.

Through practice and paying attention, we cultivate the awareness to know the difference between our own inner voice and the inner voice that has been placed there by others. Are we listening to our Small Self, which has been influenced by other people's views, values, and voices, or is it the voice of our Soul? How do we strengthen the voice of our Soul that speaks to us through intuition and inner knowing? Here are a few things you can do to cultivate an intuitive way of being:

1. Spend time alone with yourself, whether that be through walking in nature, meditating, bubble baths, or yoga.
2. Develop an awareness of your thoughts and feelings.
3. Let go of the need to "figure it out" and trust that when you're open, the answers will come.
4. Ask for "signs" and help from a place beyond the material world and your logical mind. Ask lots of questions and then let go in order to receive the answers.
5. Know that intuition will come in the form of snippets of information, messages, feelings, dreams, signs, and so on. It becomes a puzzle that, over time and with patience, slowly comes together.
6. Keep a journal to keep track of what you notice.
7. Allow yourself to play and be curious.

As we become more skilled at tuning in to our inner wisdom, we need to create space to be imperfect and make mistakes. I learned this powerful lesson in my own life a couple of years ago. My Soul was calling for growth, expansion, and to be of service. In response to this call, I applied and was admitted to a program to get a graduate degree and become a psychotherapist.

My inner voice was telling me that I needed to do this to be credible and do the type of work that I'm meant to do in the world. I packed my suitcase one hot summer day and drove three hours to Edmonton for my first intensive week of classes. As the week progressed, I had a deep inner knowing that this wasn't the program for me. I just knew. My gut was telling me that this was a definite NO, but my head argued that I'd already spent so much time, energy, and money that I shouldn't give it up. I knew that it was other people's voices that were drowning out my Soul. My Soul knew that I could become a spiritual teacher and mentor without a graduate degree, but my Small Self was fearful. I also had misbeliefs that more education and another degree would mean that I was "enough" and "worthy." My decision to go back to school was in service of my Small Self and not my Soul. It was confusing because the inner desire to grow and learn was coming from my Soul, but my response was to meet the needs of my Small Self and not my Soul. Was that a failure? Absolutely not. It was a powerful lesson, and through trial and error, I learned to become intimately aware of my inner wisdom and the difference between my Small Self and my Soul.

Over time, as I cultivated and learned to trust my intuition, I began to realize that it was a constant companion. It would let me know whether I was on the right road or headed the wrong way. It had been with me all along, and I just hadn't realized it. One of my clients put it this way, "I remember when I began teaching yoga, I had tears in my eyes. I just knew I was meant to be doing this. I just had this inner knowing. I had found my joy. There were times when I needed to take different jobs like a retail position and I just knew it wasn't right for me. I felt no satisfaction or fulfillment and I would feel really tired all the time. I knew I needed to make a change even though it was scary and when I did, I felt a lightness come over me. I was scared about not having enough money, but I knew it was what I needed to do."

Connecting with Spirit and Non-Physical Beings

As the voices of other people and our past conditioning play less of a role in guiding our decisions, we begin honing our skills in communicating with and being in the flow of the life force of a higher intelligence. Our inner wisdom becomes our guide as we open ourselves up to looking inside ourselves for answers. A relationship with our Soul means we are gaining access to a higher intelligence that expresses itself through us. A part of connecting with our Soul revolves around a curiosity and experimentation with communicating with Spirit, and non-physical beings.

Over the past several years, I've connected with angels and spirit guides through feelings, messages in songs, books, and angel cards. I had my deceased grandmother visit me in a dream, enabling me to release the guilt that I had carried for not being with her at the end of her life. I had my deceased mother-in-law visit me through random smells in my home. I had my young nephew Andy, who died suddenly, send messages through songs and photographs.

The first real intentional communication with non-physical beings came when I began getting curious about angels. I attended a weekend retreat with my girlfriends and put a bid in a silent auction item for an angel card reading. I thought, *What the hell*. At the time, I was curious about angels but didn't really believe they existed. A few weeks later, I got on a Skype call with the "angel lady." During the hour, the angel lady used cards to share some messages that supposedly came from my angels. While it seemed interesting to me, I went away thinking, *That was entertaining, but nothing proved to me that angels exist.*

More valuable than the actual reading was the information the "angel lady" gave to me about how I could communicate with angels myself. She said the biggest thing I had to do in order to receive messages from angels is to ask for them. The angels aren't going to help or interfere if we don't ask for help. This opened the door for me to begin playing with communication with angels and non-physical beings by asking for signs.

My first sign came at 4:44 AM when I was jostled out of a deep sleep, as if something or someone was nudging me. I noted the time because I glanced at the clock, but didn't think a great deal about it until the next night when the same thing happened, again at 4:44. Now I was a bit more curious but still not ready to say *maybe these are my angels or spirit guides communicating with me.* The next day, I sat down to do my regular meditation and set the timer that I use. It's not unusual for me to open my eyes periodically during the meditation to peek at the remaining time. As I glanced at the timer, my heart skipped a beat with 4:44 remaining. Now this really had my attention. After a few more 444's revealed themselves to me on license plates, a gas receipt, and my odometer, I turned to Google to find out what this message meant.

Angel number 444, according to *Joanne Sacred Scribes* website (http://sacredscribesangelnumbers.blogspot.ca) means, "You have nothing to fear in regard to your life, work and Divine life purpose and Soul mission. When you take positive actions towards your highest intentions, aspiration and goals, the Universe works in your favor and helps you to establish solid foundations and advances you along your path. Know that the angels surround and support you, encouraging you to keep up the good work you have been doing." As I read, a warm glow spread through my entire body. I had been working hard and following what I believed was my path to share meditation and mindfulness to others to support them in a new way of being. This confirmation from the angels made me smile. Not only because it felt like a group of non-physical beings cheering me on, but also because it was confirmation coming from my Soul and a higher source of intelligence. I was making a huge shift from needing confirmation from other people, who were neither able nor meant to provide it, to relying on an inner knowing that came from deep within me and from my spiritual support team.

One of the most valuable lessons I learned was related to asking for guidance and then being open to receive it. I had been keeping a journal specifically for messages, signs, synchronicities or coincidences. The more I asked, noticed, and wrote things down, the more signs I received. I had opened the tap to a whole new world of knowing that had been shut off and now was beginning to flow. Martha Graham, an American modern dancer and choreographer wrote the following as quoted by Agnes de Mille; I have it posted by my desk as a constant reminder to keep this channel open:

> "There is vitality, a life force, an energy, a quickening that is translated through you into action, and because there is only one of you in all of time, this expression is unique. And if you block it, it will never exist through any other medium and it will be lost. The world will not have it. It is not your business to determine how good it is nor how valuable nor how it compares with other expressions. It is your business to keep it yours clearly and directly, to keep the channel open. You do not even have to believe in yourself or your work. You have to keep yourself open and aware to the urges that motivate you. Keep the channel open..." (1991, p. 264).

The "urges that motivate you" are the signposts that guide us on our life's path. They are inner signposts that are unique to each of us and can only be expressed through us. We are meant to tune into these inner urges and then act on them. For many women, it's an inner pull to make some changes in our lives towards living in alignment with what we know to be true but may be afraid to act on. It is through this channel that our intuition speaks to us. Intuition bridges the gap between our material world and the spiritual dimension of our lives. It is a close and constant companion for those of us on our spiritual journey.

Around the same time that I was developing and learning to trust my intuition, I was becoming curious about prayer. I wanted to learn how to communicate directly with Spirit and, as Martha Graham said, "keep the channel open." I was finding that more and more of us identify ourselves as spiritual but not religious. We want a connection with Spirit, but don't know how to make that connection. There are also many women who have grown up with religious doctrines and ideas who have found that their prayer practices became mechanical rather than meaningful. In order to feed and hear our Souls, we are being called to find a way to commit to or begin a practice where we communicate with an intelligent life force. It doesn't matter how we do it, it just matters that we do it.

Prior to my transformation, I hadn't given much thought to prayer. I really had no idea what it was, apart from talking to Spirit. In many ways I was grateful for not having any preconceived ideas because when I did begin communicating on an almost daily basis, it became meaningful for me. If I was confused about anything in my life and needed direction, I would form a question and ask for help. I kept it simple and genuine, recognizing that I was asking for guidance or direction in relation to my Soul and not my Small Self with its desire for more "things." The answers or messages came in the way of books, people, creative ideas, dreams, an inner voice, synchronicities, or any number of other ways. We learn to ask for direction and then let go, trusting the answers will come when they are ready. You may ask questions such as:

> *How may I be of service?*
> *What do you need from me?*
> *How can I best support someone who is having a hard time?*
> *Please show me the way to let go of this anger that I feel.*
> *What am I meant to learn from this situation?*
> *What is my heart's desire?*
> *What is my body trying to tell me?*
> *Who am I beyond the roles that define me?*
> *What is the next step that I'm meant to take?*
> *What is my Soul telling me?*

People often wonder what the difference is between prayer and meditation. From my perspective, meditation enables us to settle our minds in order to create a fertile environment to receive inspiration from our higher intelligence. It enables us to become aware of our inner landscape so that we can tell the difference between whether an idea or thought is arising from our Soul or our Small Self. Some people say that prayer is talking to Spirit, while meditation is listening. I really don't think it matters that much. The point is to create enough space, silence and quiet moments in our lives and then to communicate in some way with something larger than us.

As we begin to connect with our intuition and inner knowing, we realize that it has been there all along. We had just forgotten how to listen or we hadn't created the space necessary to tune in. For women, there are a number of situations that commonly trigger our inner navigation system to let us know that we may be getting off track. One of the most common triggers is the feeling we're being pulled between our roles and our Souls.

The Pull Between Your Roles and Your Soul

Perhaps one of the biggest challenges for women is the pull between the intuitive knowing of the Soul and the mind games we play about our roles. I first heard about the idea of "rejoining role and Soul" in *A Hidden Wholeness: The Journey Toward An Undivided Life,* by Parker Palmer. Palmer explains that the divided life is a wounded life and reminds us of "the painful gap between who we most truly are and the role we play in the so-called real world" (2004, p. 15). The divided life is one that feels misaligned when our roles don't align with our Souls. This can include our careers and/or the balancing of roles that happen within our families.

Like many new mothers, I was a mixed bag of emotions when Erika was born thirty-one years ago. I was beyond grateful to have this beautiful, healthy baby girl, but at the same time, I was overwhelmed, tired, and totally in the dark about how I was going to balance the roles of being a mom, wife, daughter, friend etc. and still continue the nursing career that was a calling for me. At the time, I had no idea that what I experienced was this push and pull between my role and my Soul. I didn't know how to balance my Soul's calling to be a nurse with my desire to be a "good" mom.

As I grappled with these questions and my confusion, Mark was busy fulfilling his role to be the provider for the family. Looking back, I can now see that the challenge we were both operating from was a belief system about what it meant to be a "good" man and a "good" woman. The problem was that my Soul needed a different balance in our roles. My Soul needed for each of us to contribute to the safety and security of the family and for each of us to also contribute to the nurturing and running of the household.

I wasn't able to see any of that at the time, and so we carried on the roles that had become part of our collective unconsciousness about what was expected of men and women. I fulfilled my role to the best of my ability at the time, and so did Mark. What ended up happening was that I slowly lost my Soul in the process of fulfilling the roles that were deeply ingrained in me. As for Mark, while he became materially successful, his Soul also paid a huge price because in the process of playing his role of a successful business man to be the bread winner, he lost his Soul and experienced so much stress that his health suffered.

The problem with honoring our roles—whether within families or careers—at the expense of our Souls, is that there is always a price to pay. That price is our emotional, physical, and spiritual health. It's like our roles haven't caught up with our Souls. The roles where men are responsible for security, providing, and bringing home the bacon while women nurture and care for the children and aging parents, are not necessary anymore. And not only are they not necessary, but they're sapping our Souls and creating imbalances within us, that are creating imbalances in the outer world.

Women are being called to reunite their roles with their Souls and then replace the beliefs that are holding us back with new beliefs. This is where we need the ability to tap into our inner wisdom and our inner knowing, so that we can connect with our Souls and understand what they need from us. One thing for sure is that it is different for every woman. Some women's Soul path is to stay home and create a stable home, while other women are meant to express themselves in different ways. The challenge is that we have a society that values materialism over most other things and therefore, the roles that align with materialism, make sense to people and our Soul-health takes a back seat.

One of the most common things I heard women say thirty years ago and still hear women say today is, "I really don't have the luxury to stay home, even if I wanted to, because we need the money." While for some people this is true, for others what they're really saying is, "I need more money." While we all need a certain amount of money to survive and be comfortable, there's a certain point where more money doesn't bring greater fulfillment or meaning to our lives. This is where the Soul comes in. The Soul needs different things to thrive, and more money and material things will never feed it. We live in a society that understands the need to work for money, but is confused if this desire is stemming from your Soul's yearning for meaning and purpose.

I work with a lot of younger women, and it seems that this pull between our roles and our Souls exists as much today as it did thirty years ago when I had my children. It was the same for my mother, who was also a nurse and wasn't able to continue working after she had her kids. At that time, the pressure and cultural norm was for women to stay home. So she did. And now at the age of 85, she feels a sense of sadness and resentment that she never felt able to respond to the call of her Soul.

Our Souls are calling us to listen in all aspects of our lives and if we don't heed that call, we experience a great deal of suffering. It's not the kind of suffering a pill can fix. It's the kind of suffering that will only be diminished when we begin to align our whole life with our Soul life. That means when we allow ourselves to be authentic and real in all our relationships, even when it feels uncomfortable; and when we know the type of work that aligns with our Soul's purpose and taking the steps towards doing it. We begin to flourish when we are aware of our roles in the context of our Souls and then make the decisions in our lives accordingly.

The turning point for many women is when we find ourselves asking, "Who am I?" This question is a sign we have begun to lose ourselves in our relationships or are being defined by the roles we play. We've forgotten we are spiritual beings and are being defined by our small sense of Self. The question can come at any time, including when we're over the honeymoon phase of a new and exciting relationship and we start to feel that somehow, we've lost the "I" in the relationship.

We may be in a partnership where we feel we need to pursue the interests of the other person so that we can maintain the connection and shared interests. We take up golf, ride on the back of a motorcycle, and compromise what we really want and desire in order to meet the needs of others. Or we may feel it's our role to care for and be helpful to others and to ensure they're happy and satisfied in the relationship.

We may also find we play a role at work in terms of the position we're in. It may be the role of nurse, teacher, lawyer, entrepreneur, or professional athlete. Whatever our work role, we make adjustments to fit in with the expectations that come with it. Then, if we have children, we enter into a whole new role, as not only are we trying to find our way as new parents to this precious little life, we're having to re-establish our roles with our partners regarding who's going to do what.

Then we have the roles with our own parents, siblings, friends, and on and on. We play a lot of roles in our lives and it is inevitable that at some point we begin to ask, "Who am I beyond these roles that have defined me?" This happens when our total focus, energy, and priorities in our lives have gone into fulfilling the roles. A young stay-at-home mom put it this way, "I love staying at home with my son, but there was part of me that was very unfulfilled. I feel like I've lost my "Self" and I don't know what I am anymore. I feel guilty saying this, because I know how lucky I am. When I talk to my husband about it, he doesn't understand and says I'm really lucky and should just feel grateful. I just keep it to myself and it feels pretty lonely at times."

When the majority of our attention, energy, and focus go into fulfilling our roles based on how we "should" be, our intuition begins to give us signals that something is wrong and that something is missing in our lives. Women who don't listen to this intuition and the inner signals being sent, end up depressed, anxious, not sleeping, addicted to food or drugs, or in relationships, jobs or situations that aren't healthy. But what does it mean when we intuitively know something is missing?

When It Feels Like Something is Missing

Many women say that they feel something is missing in life, but we often feel guilty for feeling this way because we realize how fortunate we are in our lives. *What could possibly be missing when I have so many blessings?* It becomes a catch-22. Because we're grateful, we resist and try to ignore or turn away from the feelings that can be described as yearnings, longings, and/or feeling lost or disconnected. We feel selfish because we have so much that we are grateful for.

What are these feelings and inner knowing that something is missing in your life trying to tell you? It may be your intuition telling you that you're disconnected from yourself, other people, or the intelligent life force surging through you.

For as long as women can remember, we have been so busy focused on being there for other people, that we don't know who we are. We often know more about what brings other people happiness and joy, than we do about what brings us fulfilment and joy. Maybe it's a need for more adventure, fun, spontaneity, learning, balance or self-care.

This is when your Self, the part of you that makes you—you, has gone missing. We have lost sight of our values, gifts, and what makes our hearts sing. The "I am" part of you is buried beneath a whole lot of other peoples' stuff. You're busy being a "good" person and in the process have lost touch with your Self.

This disconnection from our Soul often results in feeling distanced from others in our relationships as well. The intuitive sense that something is missing often leads us to believe that the other person is lacking something, when in fact the problem resides within us. Many women long for deep and fulfilling relationships where we can share our most intimate thoughts and feelings. We want and need a deep connection with people and desire to share our Souls with others, in safe and nourishing ways.

But the Soul is shy and it will only come out when it feels it is safe to be vulnerable. When it doesn't feel safe and we don't have Soulful relationships, there's a good chance we're going to feel something is missing in our lives. We may feel lonely and disconnected even if we have countless friends and are in a serious long-term relationship.

As we connect with our Souls and the greater life force, we cultivate different qualities within ourselves that create space for this connection to flourish. The result is a dramatic shift for those of us who are often stuck in our heads, figuring things out, and hanging on to the need to always be in control. When we are living from this small sense of Self, we are suffocating what our Soul needs to thrive, which is:

- Surrender
- Letting go
- Trust/Faith
- Higher intelligence
- Flow
- Intuition
- Creativity

- Inner wisdom
- Expansion
- Meaning
- Love
- Allowing
- Natural unfolding
- Spaciousness
- Quiet

In my own life, when I turned towards the feeling that something was missing and I created space for silence, the answers revealed themselves to me. I learned that there were things missing in a number of areas of my life. As a nurse, wife, mother, and friend, I thought I needed to put others first, and in the process, I lost my sense of Self. I also had a shy Soul and although I longed for deep, connected relationships, I was afraid to feel vulnerable. And last and probably most significant was the realization that I had no idea what it meant to be a spiritual being. I was living in a spiritual desert and my Soul was thirsty for the nourishment that comes with connection to Spirit. With this realization, I had come to the place in my journey where I had to take action and begin to align the outer aspects of my life with what I had come to know were the needs of my Soul.

Awakening Your Soul

Misbelief: Your rational, logical mind is more reliable than your intuition. You're meant to "figure things out" and try to control your life.
Truth: Your intuition is a gift from an intelligent life force that is reliable and directly linked with your inner wisdom and your Soul. Tapping into intuition is a skill you can develop. Using your rational, logical mind in service of your Soul's inner knowing, creates spiritual power.

Misbelief: You are meant to compromise who you are and what you value in order to adapt in your relationships, jobs, and lives.
Truth: You are meant to adapt your relationships, jobs, and how you spend your time to align with your values and be of service to your Soul. Your Soul will suffer if you compromise what is important to you.

Misbelief: You need to rely solely on yourself and other people to get through life.

Truth: There is an intelligent life force that flows through you and non-physical beings that have your back. They are all there to guide you when you become open to receive. You are meant to be in synch with the flow of this life force and not to swim upstream against it.

Practices/Reflections

1. Use a journal or notebook to track the insights, messages, synchronicities, coincidences, dreams, and/or creative ideas you receive.

2. There is a known link between intuition and creativity. Julie Cameron, an American teacher; author, and artist who wrote the book, *The Artist's Way,* shares a powerful exercise called, "Morning Pages", a stream-of-consciousness writing practice that will get you unstuck and help you to move into the flow. Here's a link for more information: http://juliacameronlive.com/basic—tools/morning—pages/.

3. Experiment with prayer and get curious about communicating with Spirit and non-physical beings. Play around with various prayer techniques and notice what feels right for you. If you need some help with something in your life, ask for guidance during quiet times and then let it go.

CHAPTER 8

Align Your Roles and Your Soul

And once the storm is over, you won't remember how you made it through, how you managed to survive. You won't even be sure whether the storm is really over. But one thing is certain. When you come out of the storm, you won't be the same person who walked in. That's what this storm is all about.

— Haruki Murakami

It's been six years since I stood on top of Mount Kilimanjaro. While the landscape of my life may not look that different from the outside, it has changed dramatically in many ways. There was no one moment that marked the completion of my transformation. It was a slow and gradual emergence into a new way of being. This emergence was about the emergence of my Soul. My hidden Soul, which had been overshadowed by my beliefs about what it meant to be a woman. As my Soul moved into the light, it became my guide and travel companion. I stepped into a way of being that created space for my Soul to lead the way. I was no longer willing to compromise or ignore it to be the person I thought I should be. I had stepped fully into loving and honoring the person I am and allowing the highest expression of my Self to emerge.

I was beginning to consciously create my own path and move out of Mark's footsteps and into my own. It wasn't easy. Every part of me screamed that it would be so much easier to return to the comfort of my old life, rather than forging my path into an unknown that for the first time in my life had me leading and not following. Mark and I already had a well-worn path, and stepping off of it was uncomfortable. I was spending long periods of time alone in the harsh winters of Calgary, while he was in sunny Phoenix feeling equally as lonely and uncomfortable with my new path. He wanted to be with me and I with him, but we didn't have a new way of being that felt right for both us and nourished us as both unique individuals. Mark had always been my shelter in the storm and now he was in the storm with me.

As I made the decisions to spend time in Calgary and come out of retirement in order to honor my Soul's desire to continue making a difference, I felt a pull from Mark that at times was not so subtle. He held onto the hope I would change my mind and ultimately "come to my senses," as he so desperately wanted.

For a couple of years, there existed a tension between us almost like a tug of war, as if we were waiting to see who would give in. In the past whenever this tension existed, I would be the one to give, as I couldn't bear the discomfort. This had been our pattern, and so it was natural for Mark to think: *if I hold on long enough, she'll give in.* But it was different this time, and I could sense that I wasn't about to let the fear of my Small Self take over. Compromise is necessary in a healthy relationship, but compromising your Soul is the beginning of the end, both in our relationships and in our lives. Healthy compromises include what movie or restaurant we go to, or where we go on vacation, or who makes supper. But compromising our very way of being in the world, along with our values and what makes us thrive is certain death for the Soul. Mark and I loved each other and wanted to be together, but I knew being in Phoenix was not my Soul's path and I wasn't going to flourish there; and yet, I kept wondering what would happen if Mark wasn't in Phoenix. Would he flourish or would his Soul wither?

This question haunted me as every ounce of me wanted to return to the way things were—to the familiar and comfortable. Seeing and feeling the pain I knew I caused Mark by making the decision to be away from Phoenix, and ultimately him, was almost more than I could bear. Friends, family, and other important people in my life questioned my decision and what I was doing. It would have been so much easier to just say, "Forget it, I'll go back to the way things were and give up on all of this confusing nonsense." But I knew I couldn't do that. Somehow, I needed to find a way to keep my forward momentum going.

Soulful Relationships

I came to a place in my journey when I felt I had done all the "work" on myself that I could do. As I came out of the cocoon after stripping away a lot that wasn't serving me into order to connect with my Soul, I began to turn my attention to my relationship with Mark. I realized I wasn't feeling as deeply connected to him as I'd like and that this was something I was prepared to work on. I had worked on myself, and now it was time to cultivate a relationship that hopefully fed both our Souls.

Relationship experts have identified that modern relationships have not kept pace with the evolutionary needs of couples. Many of us are operating on outdated belief systems that create havoc because they neglect our Soul. The modern-day woman is perfectly capable of surviving and thriving on her own and doesn't need someone else to complete her, protect her, or put her in a box designed to keep her in a certain place. The modern-day woman needs freedom to be herself, both inside and outside of relationships.

I came across the book, *The Self-Centered Marriage: Rebuilding Your "We" by Reclaiming Your "I."* The title of the book caught my attention because I remember asking myself, *isn't it a bad thing to be self-centered*? I was curious to read more. What I read in the book confirmed why my Soul had been having a little temper tantrum to get my attention. The author, Hal Runkel, proposed that we need a new model of marriage because the old one doesn't work anymore. The old model was based on the idea that "self-sacrifice, compromise, meeting one another's needs, and the constant quest for compatibility should be our priorities." He goes on to explain, "The greatest thing that you can do for your marriage is to learn to focus more on yourself" (2011, p. 20). "What?" I had to pause and read that over a few more times, wondering again, *Isn't that selfish?*

I was curious to read more. "Every great marriage is a self-centered marriage," Runkel continued, "because every great marriage requires *centered selves*...These two strong individuals actively work on improving themselves for the other's benefit, without necessarily depending on the other to do the same. These two are afraid of neither separation nor togetherness and work to seek a balance of both. These two pay more attention to their own behavior, which they can control, than their spouse's, which they thankfully cannot" (p. 20).

This idea, combined with the seeds previously sown in my mind by Sonia Choquette about focusing on my own life and creating space for Mark to do the same, was starting to really make sense to me. I was about to learn that my belief system had been the problem all along and not actually my relationship. And everything I thought I knew about 'us' was about to be turned upside down as Mark and I delved deeply into our relationship. But knowing we needed to make some changes and actually taking concrete steps in that direction, are two very different things.

Like many married couples, we had fallen into a habit of feeling comfortable with each other but not on the level of Soul mates. Having connected with my own Soul, I now wanted my relationship with my husband to feel like a Soul connection rather than just being roommates. We had been together ever since we were teenagers and had never done any sort of relationship work together. One morning over breakfast, I cautiously said, "I'd like to go on a marriage retreat." My heart pounded as I asked if he would join me. I was never very good at asking for what I needed, especially when I knew he wouldn't love the idea. But this time Mark knew I had been doing a lot of Soul searching, and when I explained that my request wasn't because I thought our marriage was in trouble, but because it was what I needed in order to continue my growth, he reluctantly agreed.

At this point, Mark was still spending months away in Phoenix while I remained in Calgary. We decided to meet halfway in Vancouver for a weekend retreat. We booked a lovely hotel room and settled in for the weekend. I was excited, and Mark was a good sport—but he wasn't without his share of eye rolls and comments about how I had "tricked" him into attending.

The retreat actually became the turning point in our marriage. It was where our relationship shifted from being one where two people had brought all their childhood baggage and conditioning into the marriage, to being one of two adults becoming two whole and separate individuals. It became an opportunity to connect at the levels of our hearts and Souls. The weekend created an opportunity to recognize the parts of ourselves we were bringing into our relationships. We began to see clearly how our Small Self was playing out, and as we gained greater insight into this, our shy Souls were able to appear. We were transforming our relationship into what Gary Zukav called a "spiritual partnership" that nourished us and challenged us to grow and evolve. We were shifting from a reactive, need-based relationship, to one that enabled each of us to grow spiritually, based on the unique needs of our Souls.

We had been married for thirty years when we attended the Getting the Love You Want couples weekend workshop developed by Harville Hendrix, Ph.D. I often reflect back and ask myself, *Why was that weekend so transformative for our marriage?* I believe it was because much like a mindfulness practice, we began to see things that we hadn't seen before. We developed a deep understanding of why our buttons get pushed and how we can use that to deepen our connection and growth, rather than drive us apart. We gained tools that enabled us to communicate with each other so that we could feel heard and understood. These are not skills we learn in our homes, but they are necessary to bring couples closer together.

During the workshop we explored our emotional history and how it impacts the partner we choose and the reason for our power-struggles. As described on the *Imago Relationships* website (http://imagorelationships. org), the power struggles are a natural part of love and hold the key to our deeper connections and healing.

For Mark and I, it was the first time we saw each other. I mean *really* saw each other. I realized the disconnection I felt in our relationship was because I didn't really know how or feel safe enough to show Mark the real "me." Partly because I didn't know the real me, and partly because I feared maybe he wouldn't love, like, or accept the real me. I now understood why I had felt alone in the tent at night in Mount Kilimanjaro–and why I had blamed him for my inability to connect. *If only he'd be different, then I'd be different* was a deeply ingrained belief that was not going to loosen its grip on me without a fight.

As the weekend came to a close, we both knew our relationship had transformed into something that was much deeper and more spiritual. Leaving the workshop, we strolled along the sidewalk with a soft Vancouver rain falling on us. I felt a deep sense of sadness wash over me. I reflected on the newfound connection we had experienced over the weekend and realized he'd be leaving the following morning to return to Phoenix and me to Calgary. In the middle of the sidewalk, with our hair wet and our hearts heavy, we turned towards each other and held one another tight. I began to weep. In that moment, a memory flooded back to me from our wedding night thirty years before. We'd had a similar moment as we left our wedding reception and began our life together. We stopped in the hotel corridor and we both wept. The tears on our wedding night came from a place of fear and knowing that *holy crap, we're on our own now.* It was like we were two grown-up looking children clinging onto each other for dear life. Our lives would never be the same. Thirty years later, they were tears of pure love for a journey that we had taken together.

Over supper that night, Mark turned to me and said, "I know what I want to do. I want to sell our place in Phoenix because I want us to be together. You supported my dreams for most of our married life and now it's my turn to support your dreams." I will always remember that moment as being the beginning of our new chapter in our lives and our relationship. Mark made a decision that felt right for him and our relationship. We went from having a relationship based on the commonly held belief that we were going to "complete" each other, to one based on two individuals who are whole and who come together to grow spiritually. In that moment, I shifted from being the secondary partner to being an equal partner with Mark.

In the months that followed, we sold our place in Phoenix and Mark returned to be in Calgary fulltime, while I followed through on my calling to teach meditation and mentor women to awaken their Souls. I had undergone an inner transformation and my life would never be the same; and Mark and I had undergone a transformation in our relationship. Our lives as a couple changed.

Our first thirty years of marriage had been dominated by the constant push and pull between Mark's desire for security and wealth and mine to make a difference, while balancing my roles as mother, wife, daughter, sister, and friend. We were entering the next thirty years of our relationship with a commitment to honoring ourselves as spiritual beings with our unique Souls' needs to continue growing and evolving. We had come to a beautiful place where we had both undergone a transformation on the inside that was beginning to manifest on the outside. As I look back now, it feels like a miracle to me. I began to question whether this transformation that had started with me, then rippled to Mark, then cascaded into our relationship, was unique to us. Trying to understand our own personal transformation is difficult, but then attempting to understand it in the context of a relationship can be mindboggling. Mark and I were shifting, and at the root of that shift, our values were beginning to converge.

Shifting Values

The difference in values between men and women is explored in the book *Quantum Change: When Epiphanies and Sudden Insights Transform Ordinary Lives* written by William Miller, PhD, a clinical psychologist at the University of New Mexico, and Janet C'de Baca, PhD, a research scientist in Albuquerque. The authors explain that men and women have very different values at different times in their lives. When men are living primarily to meet their Small Self needs, they most often value **wealth, adventure, achievement, pleasure, and to be respected**. In contrast, women value **family, independence, career, fitting in, and attractiveness**.

The authors then examine how mens' and womens' values change when something in their lives triggers a shift, which causes them to dramatically change their worldviews and ways of being. According to their research, when people go through this dramatic change, it completely rearranges their values–which can be confusing and unsettling. As they explain, "It is not that values were slightly modified or amended. Rather, the person's value system was often turned upside down" (2001, p. 130). The single biggest change they discovered was the value that both men and women placed on **spirituality,** which rose from the bottom third to the top for men and to third place for women. Men became less "macho and materialistic", while women experienced a drop in traditional feminine values. Family remained on both lists, but for men it moved up in importance and for women it moved from first place to twelfth place. In other words, as women begin to view themselves as spiritual beings and live in alignment with their essential Selves, they place a greater value on: **Growth, self-esteem, spirituality, happiness, generosity, personal peace, honesty, forgiveness, health, creativity, loving, and family**. This means that when women honor their Souls and shed the limiting beliefs of our Small Self, we care less about fitting in and how we look and more about growing and living in alignment with our deepest truths.

As I allowed this information to sink in, I realized it explained a great deal about the events leading up to my own transformation, as well as my experience both as an individual and in my relationship. In our earlier years, as Mark was valuing wealth and achievement with a lesser value on family (even though there was never a doubt how much he loved his family), I was balancing my top priority of family with my desire to continue a career in nursing and a life based on purpose. In short, I valued family and purpose and Mark valued wealth and being successful. It's no wonder many of us have difficulties in our relationships when our core values are very different. Whose values do you honor? While the societal tides are slowly turning, in many cases it's the values held by men that most often set the direction for our relationships and roles— at least among the women I've worked with and in my own life.

At times in our relationship, I would question the decisions Mark made (based on his value of wealth), knowing they would take him further away from what I believed was important (based on my values). This made it even more difficult for me to balance my desires for career and family. It was as if Mark's value for wealth trumped mine for family and balance. At the time, I wasn't able to see or understand this, I just felt I had to go along and be supportive. This isn't surprising in view of the value society places on wealth—or the traditional beliefs many women have about ourselves and that men have about us.

One evening as I was coming to the end of writing this book, I began talking to Mark about some of the things I was including. I shared how, prior to my transformation, I often felt like I was the secondary partner and that he seemed to hold more power in our relationship. Not because he was pushy or demanding, it was just the way it was. Or should I say, it's what I accepted and believed was the "right" way to be. He agreed with me and said, "At the end of the day, the relationship currency should be love and respect, but in actuality, it's about money and power." This statement took my breath away because not only had he acknowledged and validated what I had been feeling, but he put it in a way that hit the nail on the head. He went on to add, "The person with the money and perceived power carries more weight in the relationship. It's not the way that it should be, but it's often the way that it is."

It's no wonder my personal transformation resulted in a significant shift in both my Self and my relationship with Mark. As his worldview changed and he also began to shift, we became closer. I often have women ask, "Would this have happened if you hadn't gone on the couple's retreat?" In all honesty, I don't believe our relationship would have shifted and grown this much if we hadn't had that experience. Why? Because we all have blind spots in our relationships, just as we have blind spots within ourselves. We need to gain insights and wisdom about what healthy relationships look like. Let's face it, most of us grew up with role models that were based on outdated ways of being. For the most part, we don't need each other for survival any more, but we do need each other to grow spiritually, especially when we're being called to awaken.

As I began to live my life as directed by my Soul, I had to let go of many of the beliefs holding me back. Mark also shifted to being guided by his Soul, rather than his desire to accumulate wealth. Together, we began to change from being defined by our roles to being guided by an inner divine pull that was about meaning and purpose in life. These changes represented a new way of being for both of us. As we journeyed towards embodying wholeness, both as individuals and in our marriage, we forged a new path for ourselves that had not been travelled before. We knew there was something much larger than ourselves at work that was pulling us towards this shift in our relationship—a shift that was about the realization that we needed to change the dance and not get a new dance partner as many people do. We began taking turns leading in our relationship. We knew there would be times when we stepped on each other's toes, and that was okay. This dance together was leading us towards wholeness as unique human beings who were discovering a way to balance the material and spiritual aspects of our being.

After we've undergone a transformation and are living from a more authentic place, the shift in what we value often impacts who we choose to hang out with and how we spend our time. Many women describe how they're not as interested in superficial friendships and conversations. They desire deeper and more meaningful friendships that are based on valuing quality, rather than quantity and on coming together to connect at a more spiritual level. They're open to supporting each other when asking questions such as: *Why did this situation push my buttons? What am I meant to learn? How am I meant to grow? Is this my Small Self speaking to me or is this my Soul and a message from Spirit? How can I cultivate the spiritual values of compassion and acceptance even in the most challenging situations?*

As we ask these questions and receive answers, we move forward by aligning our lives around the messages we receive in order to express our Selves based on our highest calling.

With this shift, many women wonder what happens with spouses, partners, and friends who don't accept who you've become. This is probably the biggest concern that holds women back. The key here is the realization that we're not becoming someone "new." Rather, we're becoming more of who we were always meant to be. Evolving and expressing ourselves more fully and authentically means some people will naturally fall away. Our job is to know who we are and what we value, and to live in alignment with that. Others, including our partners and friends will need to make their own decisions based on whether they will grow with us or want to remain in a relationship that feels constricted and, to put it bluntly, stagnant. Women who are awakening will never thrive in a stagnant relationship. The rate of growth varies and fluctuates, but even if it's subtle, there is always movement.

Returning to Wholeness

Once you have touched that inner space and connected with your Soul, you're called to find the courage to arrange your whole life around your highest Self. You are making a conscious choice to let go of the divided life you may have been living prior to your transformation. As we bring our lives back into alignment, we begin to walk through the world feeling and being completely aligned with the truth of who we are. Embodying this wholeness means that we take the steps to align the outer aspects of our lives with the truth of what our Soul needs to thrive. We begin to notice whether the work we are doing is in alignment with our highest calling and makes use of our gifts and talents. We explore whether our relationships are nourishing, and we create opportunities to grow and evolve as unique individuals. We have a desire for our bodies to feel vital and in balance, with a resilience that allows us to thrive under the normal stresses of our busy lives. As the Canadian poet Rupi Kaur so beautifully expressed:

"It is when I stopped searching for home in others and lifted the foundations of home within myself I found there were no roots more intimate than those between a mind and body that have decided to be whole" (2017, p. 215).

Embodying wholeness is the primary purpose of our lives. Our Soul is calling us to become an integrated whole and to remove the barriers that keep us separated from our divine essence. This awareness came through me one day when I was on a slow and contemplative walk along a path in a nearby treed park on a sunny spring day. I had been on this inner journey for some time, and as I walked I asked, "What, ultimately, is the purpose of my life? Why am I here?" I didn't expect an answer because I had been asking this question a lot over the past several months and never seemed to receive an answer. But this day was different. I remember vividly the place on the path were the answer came to me. I heard a little voice that said, "Your primary purpose is to become whole, which means to align your life with the intelligence that is guiding you every moment of every day. You are meant to heal your life. Your purpose isn't to "fix" other people, it's to work on your own life and create space for others to work on theirs." The message I received that day has been a guiding light for me ever since.

Over the course of my journey, I have come to understand that everything in the universe is organizing, encouraging, and calling us to return to wholeness. This wholeness is ultimately a return to living in expansion, openness, and balance in life, rather than in constriction and fear. A shift to this way of being always begins on the inside where it's less obvious, but we get to a point in the journey where we are called to ensure that the outer expression of our life is aligned with the inner changes we have undergone. It is through the inner journey of connecting with ourselves that we strip away what doesn't serve us in order to become fully aware of who we are, what we value, what our dreams are, and how we're meant to contribute in the world.

For many of us on this journey towards wholeness, we rely on the meditation and mindfulness practices explored in this book to create the conditions inside of us needed for healing. It is the intelligent life force of which we are a part that facilitates the healing within us, which means that it's not us humans who do the healing. Think about what happens when a person breaks their arm. They go to the emergency room to have a doctor put the bone back into alignment. The doctor aligns the bone but doesn't heal it. What heals the bone? Nature or an intelligent universe heals the bone. In the same way, when we bring our thoughts, feelings, emotions, beliefs, and actions into alignment with Spirit and spiritual laws, we begin to heal and in this process we become whole. We let go of the conditioning and beliefs about who we believe we should be and align our lives with our Souls, which is who we're meant to become. As we reorganize our inner world, our outer world will fall into place. The reorganizing isn't easy, but it is necessary to become whole.

A core message of Roshi Joan Halifax, a Buddhist teacher and founder of Upaya Zen Center in Santa Fe, New Mexico, is "strong back, soft front." Just sit for a moment and let that concept really sink into your being. What does it mean to you? Joan Halifax explains that having a strong back and soft front "is about the relationship between equanimity and compassion. 'Strong back' is equanimity and your capacity to really uphold yourself. 'Soft front' is opening to things as they are." She introduced this practice in relation to being with the dying, but I have integrated it into my own life and my work with women. Imagine being a woman who, no matter what comes along in your life, is able to maintain an open, compassionate heart while simultaneously having a strong backbone. It's really what awakening your Soul is all about.

When we cultivate a strong back and soft front within ourselves, we are embodying wholeness. We unite all parts of ourselves into one being and then walk through the world living in alignment with that awareness of who we are. We unite the qualities traditionally associated with the feminine way of being—gentleness, empathy, and sensitivity—with those that are traditionally associated with the masculine way of being—courage, independence, and assertiveness. We weave together the spiritual qualities of compassion, kindness, love, forgiveness, acceptance, understanding, and grace with qualities that are required to remain grounded during difficult times.

This concept of strong back, soft front took on a new and evolved meaning for me as I began to integrate it into my daily meditation practice. I realized that throughout my life I had cultivated a soft front and a soft back. I knew how to be compassionate, loving, and forgiving, but I hadn't cultivated a strong back to support the soft front. I had never given myself permission to uphold myself because I had always put other people first. I had what is commonly called, "the disease to please." Without the strong back, we find ourselves closing our hearts. This practice enables us to maintain a strong back and stand firmly in our inner knowing that change, while uncomfortable, is necessary to bring our lives into alignment with our Souls.

Getting in The Flow

Many women who enter into the cocoon to connect with the deepest parts of themselves come out with a way of being that feels different. We have shifted from the frenetic pace of life where a successful day is measured by how much we got done, to a way of being that is in greater alignment with nature and the natural flow of life. We realize the importance of carving out space in our lives for alone time, silence, and contemplation in order to connect with our Souls. I often say that I went into the cocoon believing I was an extrovert, because of the great lengths I went to be busy and actually avoid my Self, and I came out more of an introvert.

When we organize our lives around this balance and take our cues from nature and Spirit, we find we are caught up in a powerful flow instead of resistance. We stop trying to force things and literally "go with the flow." As we bring our lives back into alignment with the natural rhythms, we balance the masculine/feminine, heaven/earth, outer/inner, self/other, I/we, being/doing, intellect/intuition, left brain/right brain, speaking/listening, and light/dark. We are ultimately balancing our way of being that includes both our human and our spiritual natures.

The ancient spiritual wisdom of the Tao Te Ching, translated by Stephen Mitchell, expressed this flow beautifully in the following passage:

"There is a time for being ahead,
a time for being behind;

a time for being in motion,
a time for being at rest;
a time for being vigorous,
a time for being exhausted;
a time for being safe,
a time for being in danger.
The master sees things as they are,
without trying to control them.
She lets them go their own way,
and resides at the center of the circle" (1999, p. 29).

Our new way of being is about being in tune with our "time." *What is it our Soul needs in this moment? What needs to come back into balance in our lives? Are we going against the flow and making things more difficult for ourselves?* Our efforts to control how things unfold ends up creating resistance, which is the fastest way to block the flow and get out of synch with the natural rhythms of our lives. The inner resistance we feel in response to the moments in our lives is usually related to one thing: **fear**, and more specifically, **fear of change**.

There is no doubt about it; change is scary and often difficult. Even if our Soul is screaming for something to change in our lives, it doesn't mean that change will feel comfortable. What does feel comfortable is staying in our comfort zones. It's interesting that the Universe is organized around change and yet every part of our Small Self or ego wants us to stay the same and *not* change. This push and pull between what our Soul needs from us and what our Small Self needs is something you'll need to master when you set out on a spiritual journey. To begin living lives that are deeply meaningful and fulfilling, we need to recognize and accept that fear and resistance will be our close and constant companion. Listening exclusively to our Small Self will result in the starvation of our Souls.

One of the biggest barriers to getting into the flow is our natural tendency and need to have it all figured out before we get started. Society bombards us with the masculine way of creating, which is to set a goal and then take steps along a linear path to achieve the goal. As Thomas Merton, a Catholic writer, theologian and mystic said, "You do not need to know precisely what is happening, or exactly where it is all going. What you need is to recognize the possibilities and challenges offered by the present moment, and to embrace them with courage, faith, and hope."

Courage, faith, and hope are exactly what Beth was looking for when I met her. Beth was in her late thirties when she knew something was wrong in her life. From the outside looking in, she had the "perfect" life. She had a stable career with a great income and benefits working as an HR consultant in an oil and gas company, a husband whom she loved, a one-year-old daughter, and a comfortable home in a nice neighborhood.

After a thirteen-month maternity leave, Beth returned to work. Shortly after her return she began to feel like something was wrong. She couldn't put her finger on it, but she just didn't feel like her old self. She was tired all the time, felt hopeless, and no longer found any joy at work. She couldn't concentrate and cried at the drop of a hat. She was getting sick frequently with sinus infections she couldn't seem to shake. This woman who had been the strong one, always in control, the one people called "Little Miss Sunshine," was feeling lost, confused, and drained both physically and emotionally. She felt as if she was losing her mind.

Every day became a struggle, and after a while, Beth realized she had no choice but to take a six-month leave from work to figure it out. She intuitively knew what she was experiencing wasn't a depression that was going to be fixed by some pill. Although she couldn't explain why, she found herself Googling meditation and mindfulness. She had an inner sense that this was the route she was meant to go. That's when she reached out to me.

Beth arrived at my office as a tall, beautiful, well-dressed professional woman who exuded confidence. As she began to share her story, however, the confident veneer fell away and the tears started flowing. Although she didn't feel stuck, she had no idea what was wrong and didn't know how to go about making changes. *What needed to change? What was all of this telling her? How could she get her inner sparkle back?*

As Beth began to do her inner work by integrating daily meditation and mindfulness practices into her life, she began to experience a shift. She began to reconnect with herself and as she did, she came face to face with the things that were starving her Soul. She learned she had some beliefs about what it meant to be strong and successful, and that she had never really learned how to feel her feelings and allow herself to be vulnerable. Her grandmother told her that, "Money was not important, but you can't live without it." She knew this was a message that resonated with her, but how was it relevant to what she was going through?

Beth began to question whether she would ever be happy in her corporate job. She felt torn between the security of a stable job where she was miserable, and being pulled to move in a different direction. How could she give up her job for a path yet to be determined? As the leave progressed, however, and Beth made space for the inner journey of being in a cocoon of self-discovery and transformation, the veil of hopelessness and deep stress began to lift. She began to feel more energized, her sinus infections went away, and her mind became clearer.

Beth returned to work with a newfound resilience. She began to listen and trust her inner knowing. She questioned whether the corporate environment was a fit for her Soul. Her intuition told her she needed something more fulfilling where she would make an impact on people's lives, and she began to question what her life's purpose might be and how she could use her gifts to make a difference.

Her Soul was calling her to make a shift, but she also knew her need for security was important, so she began taking courses on the side to pursue a career in life coaching. Although she was still working full-time in her corporate job and was busy raising her daughter, she knew she was on the right path. As she said to me, "I do need to keep going on my path and won't let this fear of changing directions distract me. I'm being pulled from inside and know that I need to listen to my heart." She was on the road to connecting with her deeper purpose.

What Beth and so many other women experience when we don't listen to our intuition and honor our inner wisdom are significant physical and emotional issues. Soul pain causes stress, and it won't go away until we listen to it. For Beth, the pain made itself known in recurrent infections, a mind that wasn't as sharp as it had been, and a feeling of hopelessness. Beth was a strong woman and knew she needed to face this head on. Others may make different choices and try to avoid the pain and discomfort by over-eating, drinking, shopping, and other equally distracting and numbing things.

As I journeyed with Beth, I was reminded that while our life circumstances were different, our stories were very much the same. We both had Soul pain because we weren't acknowledging our divine path. This Soul pain and neglect were resulting in physical and emotional suffering. We both needed to "cocoon" for a period of time to connect with our inner wisdom and listen to the whispers from our Soul. When we connected with our Soul and became clearer about the direction we were meant to go, it was time for action.

The universe responds to action. Taking one step and then the next step in response to our inner wisdom, starts the process of creating a fully aligned life. In *The Seven Spiritual Laws of Success: A Practical Guide to the Fulfillment of Your Dreams,* Deepak Chopra outlines how the spiritual laws work in our lives. As Chopra explains, "The physical laws of the universe are actually this whole process of divinity in motion, or consciousness in motion. When we understand these laws and apply them in our lives, anything we want can be created, because the same laws that nature uses to create a forest, or a galaxy, or a star, or a human body can also bring about the fulfillment of our deepest desires" (1994, p. 5). This force in the universe is directly connected to our Soul. It feels like an inner urge or knowing. We sense we're pulled or drawn in a certain direction that we can't always understand or explain. Listening and being guided by this inner pull requires a level of trust that can at times be challenging, especially when our intellectual mind gets involved.

In contrast to this energy that Deepak Chopra refers to as "spirit in action" we have another force that is pulling us back, much like gravity. This resistance arises from our ego or Small Self, which despises change and operates under the illusion that it can be in control of everything. It manifests as a fear of the unknown, and it has us put on the brakes and either consciously or subconsciously decide to resist the intelligent life force pulling and urging us forward. When we resist or turn our back on the urges and inner calling to grow and evolve, we stay stuck.

As we face our fears and move forward in spite of them, we move into the flow of a Soul-inspired life. With each step we ask ourselves: *Is the direction I'm moving in and the choices I'm making in service of my Small Self, or are they in service of my Soul and my spiritual life path?* The answer to this question will always appear in our bodies. Through the cultivation of mindfulness, we become skillful at tuning into the wisdom of our body as we navigate our way forward. Our body will let us know if our gut is telling us that we've gotten off track and we need to make some course corrections.

Actions that feel expansive, open and like an inner bell of excitement have been rung, are the cue we're moving in the right direction.

The Fully Awake Soul's "To Be and Do" List

Some people have the idea that to be fully awake means we go through life in a state of "being" and very little "doing." We're so much in the flow that we just sit back and let life happen to us. I think it's more accurate to say that the awakening Soul balances the being and doing and sets the intention to be fully present during the "doing" phase. We view ourselves as co-creators with something larger than ourselves. This alignment with an intelligent life force turns us into manifesting machines, but we're manifesting in service of the Soul and not the Small Self.

The biggest shift in creating a new way of being is about where we put our energy—and about the value we place on balancing the needs of our Soul with the needs of our roles. I've always been a "to do" list kind of girl, and I always will be; however, the nature of things that go on my to do list has shifted. Living a life that feels whole and that nourishes both the material and spiritual aspects of ourselves involves a continual awareness of three areas in our lives. These three things make up what I lovingly call the trinity for the Soul: **Feeling alive, feeling connected, and feeling like we make a difference**. The specific and unique ways that we bring life to these areas will vary, but the underlying need to feed these aspects of ourselves is found in all of us.

Feeling Alive and Vibrant: We all want to feel fully alive and thriving in our lives. It may be that we need to drink more water, exercise, eat healthier, sign up for a course, paint, journal, dance, sing, do yoga, be mindful, walk in nature, have lunch with a friend, play with the dog, write a book, take a nap, or so on. We ask ourselves *what do I need in order to feel vibrant and fully alive?* It's interesting that the answer to the question about what we need often changes over time. When I had young children at home, my answer would have been very different than it is at this stage of my life. When we ask the question and let go of the "should," we will hear an answer.

Susan, a young mom with two toddlers, put it this way, "In order to feel my best, I have come to rely on meditation, self-compassion, yoga, music, laughing and dancing. I have always loved to learn and so I'm always taking a course or a workshop or something. I did not have a model for healthy self-care growing up and at first I struggled with feeling guilty for spending time on myself. I quickly realized that there was no way I was going to be the best wife, mother, friend, colleague or daughter without some serious self-care."

Feeling Connected. We are hardwired for connection and when any of the important connections are frayed in our lives, we won't thrive. We need to feel connected to ourselves, with others in a meaningful way, and with something greater than ourselves. All three must be in balance in order for our Soul to thrive and embody wholeness. They are interrelated and interdependent.

In order to have deep and meaningful connections with other people, we need to have deep and meaningful connections with ourselves. If we feel something is missing in our relationships, it is a reflection that something is missing and not connected within ourselves. If I love, honor, and cherish myself, I will attract people into my life that love, honor, and cherish me. The connection with our Self becomes the doorway to thriving in our relationships and connecting with something greater than us.

Whether we acknowledge it or not, we as human beings have a mysterious and miraculous relationship with something larger than ourselves. Susan explained beautifully how it was through her connection with both herself and something larger than herself, that she was able to take down the walls around her heart that prevented her from connecting with others:

> "I have found that the inner journey is the most important one you will ever embark on. My inner world is where my power, my drive and my life force are. Connecting with my inner world helped me to know who I am truly meant to be. Not what others expect of me. It has helped me sort out my priorities and what really matters to me. When I am not walking in my truth, I feel dull and heavy. I also need my connection to what I call God. I love the analogy of a lamp. A lamp can only shine when it is plugged in. Meditating, prayer, breathing and music are all ways I have learned to plug in. I have learned to unlock my ability to create my own happiness."

Susan's analogy of a lamp that needs to be plugged in to shine is a powerful one. She has found that this connection to something that is greater than herself (what she calls God), has been a source of inspiration and strength. When we believe we are connected to an intelligence in this universe and we learn how to be in the flow with it, our lives take on a new dimension of mystery, curiosity, and fun.

Feeling like we make a difference. At the end of our lives, most of us want to believe that we have in some way made a difference. That our lives mattered. This is truly what makes our Souls sing and is part of the waking up process. How we make a difference and what that looks like is very different from woman to woman. How I made a difference when I was younger is different than how I define that now.

The challenge for most of us is connecting with what that difference is meant to be. Where does the source of inspiration for that difference come from? From the connection that we have made with a higher intelligence. When we are moved to make a difference based on the universe speaking through us, we are on the path to living fully and feeding our Souls.

As one of my clients said, "It's as if I'm an instrument for something bigger. The work I did for 20 years that really didn't light me up, has prepared me for what I'm doing now. I feel called and pulled to create this new program. I wish I didn't have to go through all the pain to get here and find my way. But I'm on my path."

When we're being pulled to make a difference, we are being asked to listen, follow, and allow it to unfold. Making a difference is a moment-to-moment thing, and as we surrender to the reality that we will likely not have it all figured out before we get started, we find inner peace. We commit to taking the next step that feels right and to being guided from within.

We become a human being who is inspired by our Soul and is thriving. We begin to focus our lives around what makes us feel fully alive and what brings meaning to our lives. We cultivate a deep connection with others, an intelligent life force, and ourselves. Perhaps one client said it best when she said, "This journey has given me the gift of presence, of calm, of excitement, of satiation, of energy, of contentment. I have reignited my spark."

As I mentioned at the very beginning of this book, my journey of awakening began with a Soul hunger that landed me in a counselor's office. At that time, I didn't need psychological support as much as I needed a trusted mentor and guide who understood how the Soul is meant to be uncovered. I needed someone who knew about transformation and how to usher a new way of being into the world. I needed to know that what I was about to embark on, in awakening my Soul, was not only necessary but a beautiful process of becoming more and more my Self. I needed reassurance that it would be the most important and valuable journey of my life—and although it would be scary at times, I would eventually thrive.

Women need to know that the beautiful, deep, scary, adventurous, and necessary dance with our Selves, our relationships, and a higher intelligence will unlock the mysteries of our Souls. All of us have the answers within us to guide us down a path that leads us closer to who we were always meant to become. When we are brave enough to let the life force flow through us, we will be led step-by-step to exactly where we're meant to be. We will dance to the beat of our own drums. And we will embody women who are living deeply awakened lives.

Awakening Your Soul

Misbelief: Success is measured by how many things you accomplish in a day, how much money you make, how many friends you have, how many Facebook likes you have, how exotic your last vacation was.
Truth: From the Soul's perspective, success is measured by the degree to which you live your life based on the highest expression of who you are at the core of your being.

Misbelief: You must work hard to get what you want.
Truth: Life isn't meant to be a struggle. The universe is organizing around your highest expression, and when you let go and align yourself with the natural flow, you'll find yourself being guided along, one step at a time.

Misbelief: An intelligent life force exists outside of you.
Truth: You are a unique expression of Spirit that communicates through your Soul. Even though you're connected with all other beings, there is no one else in this universe that is **you**. You are meant to let that life force flow through you and guide you as you move through life accepting what is, while embracing who you are becoming.

Practices/Reflections

1. Either alone or with Soulful friends, do a vision board that is in service of your Soul.

2. Shift your "to do list" to the trinity for the Soul. What do you need to feel fully alive, connected, and like you're making a difference?

3. Allow your days to unfold in a natural rhythm that balances the being with the doing and honors the fact that you are a spiritual being having a human experience.

Tips and Additional Practices

The process of transformation and awakening your Soul is full of twists, turns, and uncertainty. Looking back, there were many things I wish I knew as I embarked on the journey to bring my outer life into alignment with my inner truths. The words of wisdom in this book have been compiled to assist you on your journey. They represent what you may need to be mindful of as you come face to face with the misbeliefs that may be preventing you from fully thriving in all aspects of your life.

The following are **Ten Tips for the Awakening Woman**:

1. Be mindful of the different hungers that exist within you. Become intimately familiar with the difference between your Soul speaking to you and your Small Self speaking. The Small Self is louder and often more convincing, which often causes the Soul, which is very shy, to fade into the background.
2. Be mindful of losing yourself in your roles, whatever they may be. Your Small Self will say that your identity and self-worth are tied to your roles, while your Soul wants and needs to be known beyond the roles that define you. Roles will always change, and when you lose yourself in them, you will lose your very essence. Women thrive when they honor their Souls within their roles.
3. Be mindful of creating space for your Soul. The Small Self flourishes in the face of distractions, busyness, and focusing on others' lives, while the Soul craves space. When given space, the Soul speaks

through intuition, inner knowing, longing, and an inner pull for growth and expansion.

4. Be mindful of the fact that to connect with our Souls, we need to clear away the clutter and garbage that dims our light and inner sparkle. This involves the ability to forgive and to work with limiting beliefs. Be willing to see things that may have been hidden.

5. Be mindful of the little voice inside your head and cultivate a relationship with yourself that is based on unconditional love, acceptance, and compassion.

6. Be mindful of and cultivate a meaningful relationship with a life force greater than yourself. Allow your life to be guided by this life force that is working through you. Create space daily to nourish this relationship and listen to your inner wisdom and intuition, and honor them above all and everyone else. Trust that the universe has your back.

7. Be mindful of setting your bar too low. You are meant to thrive and not merely survive. Feeling like you're surviving is a sign that you're living in alignment with your Small Self, whereas when you're thriving, you are aligned with your Soul.

8. Be mindful of resistance and fear when you're shifting the outer circumstances of your life to be in alignment with your Soul. Working through the fear and resistance is part of the process, and it is necessary in order to shift from living in alignment with your Small Self, to living in alignment with your Soul.

9. Be mindful of your relationship with gratitude. Learn to be grateful for the highs and lows in your life, as they are part of your Soul's path and need for growth.

10. Be mindful of the awareness that your Soul has a path and destiny to fulfill. Your destiny was determined by an intelligent universe and the greater the alignment between your Soul and your outer life, the greater will be the flow, synchronicities, and coincidences.

Seven Key Practices

As this book came to an end, I realized there were a number of practices that weren't included that may be helpful for you. While this wasn't intended to be a *how to* meditate book, there are specific tools that are helpful for every spiritual seeker to have in their toolkit. The following includes a summary of **seven practices** that were instrumental in my life and the other women in this book.

Practice #1 Simple Meditation Practice

Begin with a five-minute sitting practice. It's important to set yourself up for success. Having a meditation practice in your toolkit provides an invaluable foundation for a life where you'll thrive physically, emotionally, and spiritually. It is a powerful practice for inner peace, vibrant health, and for connecting with your Soul. A sitting meditation practice is simple when you know what you're doing. To set the stage for going deeper within ourselves, we need to shift from a body that is merely surviving, to one that is thriving.

One of the simplest ways to do that is by triggering what Dr. Herbert Benson calls the "relaxation response." Dr. Benson, a cardiologist and founder of Harvard's Mind/Body Medical Institute, is credited with demystifying meditation and bringing it into the mainstream. In his book, *The Relaxation Response,* he describes a process to shift from the "fight or flight" response to a balanced, restful state of "rest and digest."

He suggests that a few minutes, once or twice daily, can counteract the stress response and create inner peace, deep relaxation, and a healing environment in the body. The following is a simple practice that I use and teach. To download *A Beginner's Guide to Meditation* visit my website at www.bevjanisch.com.

1. Sit quietly in a comfortable position.
2. Close your eyes.
3. Bring your attention to your body and, moving from your head to your toes, allow yourself to relax the muscles in your body.
4. Now focus your attention on your breath and notice how the air moves in and out through your nose or how your chest rises and falls. You may find it helpful to count your breaths or introduce a short phrase or word with preferably no meaning.
5. When your mind wanders, gently and kindly bring it back to focus on your breath or the word. It doesn't matter how many times you need to bring it back.
6. Continue this way for your predetermined time. You may begin with five minutes and then slowly increasing the time until you're meditating for twenty minutes, twice a day.
7. Come out of your meditation slowly and then carry on with your day.

Practice #2 Gratitude

Early on in my transformation, I decided to experiment with three gratitude practices to see how I'd feel after six weeks of doing them on a regular basis. I chose these practices because they don't take a lot of time and are all supported by research in terms of reaping benefits.

1. Start a gratitude journal or include it in your existing journal. Although you can write in it any time, practicing gratitude before you drift off to sleep is powerful. Close your eyes for a couple of minutes and focus on your heart as a way of enlivening your heart's energy. Once you feel connected with your heart, open your eyes and reflect on the things throughout the day that you were grateful for. Write what comes to mind and perhaps set an intention of listing five things.
2. Pause frequently throughout the day for mindful moments that I call "instant gratitude". This involves stopping what you're doing

and bringing your awareness fully into what is going on in you and around you. Focus on the pleasant things but also the not so pleasant things. For example, this morning I was feeling anxious. You know that feeling where you have butterflies in your stomach? My stomach had lots of stuff going on, and in the moment, that I paused, I shifted my focus. Instead of pushing the anxiety away, I said "Thank you" for the awareness that something in my thoughts was triggering it. I realized I was feeling overwhelmed with the need to control things. I "leaned into" the discomfort, and with my awareness, I was able to shift my thinking and the anxiety dissolved.

3. Write a letter to someone who made a difference in your life and who may not be aware of the impact they have had on you. Create an opportunity for a special moment to give it to them. Like William Arthur Ward said, "Feeling gratitude and not expressing it is like wrapping a present and not giving it." It is a beautiful and powerful experience of connection and love.

Practice #3 Use Your Breath

Your breath is the most powerful tool you have for shifting your nervous system into a peaceful state. This is a quick and easy practice that you can do anytime, anywhere. Building these moments into your day will increase your stress resilience. It involves both visualization and deep breathing, and only takes about six seconds to stop stress in its tracks. You can use it throughout the day when you need to feel calm and relaxed. This is how you do it:

1. When you notice you're feeling tense or stressed, turn your attention into your body and release the tension in your shoulders, allowing them to drop away from your ears.
2. Imagine holes in the bottom of your feet and as you breathe in deeply imagine that the air is flowing up through your legs and your torso and filling your lungs.
3. Relax your muscles as the warm air moves up through your body.
4. Exhale by reversing the visualization as the warm air slowly moves from your lungs and back out through the holes in the soles of your feet.

Practice #4 Repeat a Phrase or Saying

When something happens such as being called into our boss's office, or our spouse pushes our buttons, or our kids are late coming home and haven't called, we begin to tell ourselves all sorts of stories. These stories often leave us feeling fearful, which triggers our flight-or-fight response and the cascade of changes in our body that I outlined previously. Taking a number of long, slow, breaths as outlined in the previous example is really powerful, as is repeating calming phrases or sayings such as: "This too shall pass. I am safe. I can do this. I am courageous. Whatever happens, I'll be okay. I am resilient." You will develop your own favorite, go-to sayings that you can draw on in the heat of the moment.

Practice #5 S.T.O.P.

Elisha Goldstein shared the S.T.O.P practice in the August 2013 issue of *Mindful Magazine.* It's a powerful practice for dealing with stressful moments in the day and mitigating the effects of stress.

S — Stop and put down what you're doing for a minute.

T — Take a few deep breaths. Following your breath with repeating "in" as you breathe in and "out" as you breathe out.

O — Observe what you are experiencing, just as it is. This includes your thoughts, feelings, and emotions, and how they feel in your body. Get curious about the experience rather than being carried away by it. Sometimes it's helpful to name what you're feeling. This helps balance our brains' emotional intensity by putting words to what we feel. There are even some brain studies that show how this naming process can reduce the feeling intensity.

P — Proceed with an action that will support you in the moment, such as taking a short walk, having a cup of tea, or listening to music.

Practice #6 Turn Worry into Prayer

I mentioned earlier that your thoughts may trigger a fight-or-flight response, just as a real threat is able to. For that reason, our tendency to worry about things that will likely never happen has an impact on our physical and emotional health. The idea of turning your worry into a prayer is a powerful one, as it creates an opportunity for you to let go of the things and situations that are beyond your control.

Some people may say, "I'm not religious, so that won't work for me." This is becoming increasingly relevant as more people are identifying themselves as spiritual and not religious. So let's just say that when you're doing this, you're turning your worry over to a higher power, the universe, the divine non-physical beings such as angels, or whatever happens to resonate with you. One of the most popular prayers that many people use is the serenity prayer: "God grant me the serenity to accept the things I cannot change, the courage to change the things I can, and the wisdom to know the difference."

Practice #7 Prayer for the Spiritually Minded

Prayer is an act of communication that can be performed by anyone with or without religious beliefs. Even if you are not sure you believe in God, you can still benefit from a daily practice of intentional communication with an intelligent life force. Prayer may be even more beneficial when it is removed from a religious setting and becomes a private, personal act that is spontaneous and not rehearsed or memorized.

Why pray? Because it will help you connect with others in the world who are suffering; because it will help you tap into the energy of an intelligent life force; and because it will cultivate love, connection to, and compassion with yourself and others.

Here are some pointers for beginning your own practice of prayer:

- Create a quiet space. Try sitting, kneeling, or even lying down in a comfortable place where you won't be disturbed.
- Calm yourself by taking a few deep breaths.
- Contemplate the concerns you have and set your intention on holding them in your heart during this time. You may want to begin with concerns for yourself, then expand to others in your life, your community, nation, planet, etc.
- Connect with the flow of energy around you. Allow yourself to sense the pulse of life and creativity that infuses everything. For some this

is called Spirit or God or the Divine, but you might simply perceive it as an energetic life force.

- Communicate either silently or aloud by naming your concern, then visualize sending your own love and compassion to that person or place. You may also visualize turning that concern over to the universe.

Whenever possible, let your prayers arise spontaneously from within you rather than planning them in advance. But if you feel insecure about this at first, here are some specific things you might pray for:

- Growth in wisdom, love, compassion, and insight for yourself and others.
- Wholeness of body, mind, spirit, and the planet.
- Peace and understanding.
- Guidance for yourself and others to make wise decisions that align with your Soul.
- Cultivating strength, courage, patience, and endurance to help you get through difficult times.
- Gratitude: let every prayer begin and end with thankfulness.

To learn more about Bev's transformational coaching program or to sign up for her Soulful newsletter visit: www.bevjanisch.com.

References

A Course in Miracles, Combined Volume (3rd ed.). (2007). Foundation for Inner Peace.

Brown, B. (2010). *The gifts of imperfection: Let go of who you think you're supposed to be and embrace who you are.* Center City, Minnesota: Hazelden Publishing.

Cameron, J. (2018). *Julia Cameron live: The artist's way.* Retrieved from http://juliacameronlive.com/basic-tools/morning-pages/.

Chopra, D. (1994). *The seven spiritual laws of success. A practical guide to the fulfillment of your dreams.* San Rafael, CA: Amber-Allen Publishing.

Choquette, S. (2013). *Tune in: Let your intuition guide you to fulfillment and flow.* Carlsbad, California: Hay House.

De Mille, A. (1991*). Martha: The life and work of Martha Graham.* New York City, NY: Random House.

Goldstein, E. (2013, May). Stressing Out? S.T.O.P. *Mindful.* Retrieved from https://www.mindful.org/stressing-out-stop/.

Gunaratana, B. (2011). *Mindfulness in plain English.* Somerville, MA: Wisdom Publications.

Halifax, J. (2017). *Upaya Institute and Zen Center*. Retrieved from https://www.upaya.org/about/roshi/.

Hanson, R., & Mendius, R. (2009). *Buddha's brain: The practical neuroscience of happiness, love & wisdom*. Oakland, CA; New Harbinger Publications, Inc.

Hay, L. (2013). *The essential Louise Hay collection*. New York, United States: Hay House, Inc.

Imago Relationships. (2016). *Getting the love you want— Couples weekend workshop*. Retrieved from http://imagorelationships.org/pub/find-a-workshop/getting-the-love-you-want-couples-weekend-workshop/.

*Insight Time*r (2018). Retrieved from https://insighttimer.com.

Kaur, R. (2017). *The sun and her flowers*. Kansas City, Missouri: Andrews McMell Publishing.

Kornfield, J. (2008). *Meditation for beginners* (Audiobook). Boulder, CO: Sounds True, Inc.

McLean, S. (2012). *Soul centered: Transform your life in 8 weeks with meditation*. United States: Hay House, Inc.

Miller, W. R., & C'deBaca, J. (2001*). Quantum change: When epiphanies and sudden insights transform ordinary lives*. New York, NY: The Guilford Press.

Mitchell, S. (1999). *Tao Te Ching: Lao Tzu*. Islington, London: Frances Lincoln Limited.

Monk Kidd, S. (2016). *The dance of the dissident daughter: A woman's journey from Christian tradition to the sacred feminine*. New York, NY: HarperCollins Publishers. (Original work published 1996).

Neff, K. (2011). *Self-compassion: The proven power of being kind to yourself.* New York, NY: HarperCollins Publishers.

Neff, K. (2018). *Self-Compassion Quiz*. Retrieved from http://self- compassion.org/test-how-self-compassionate-you-are/.

Neff, K. (2018). *Self-Compassion Break* (Audio). Retrieved from http://self-compassion.org.

Osbon, D.K. (1991). *Reflections on the art of living: Joseph Campbell companion*. New York: HarperCollins.

Palmer, P. (2004). *A hidden wholeness: The journey toward an undivided life*. San Francisco, CA: Jossey-Bass.

Paulus, T. (2000). *Hope for the flowers*. Mahwah, NJ: Paulist Press. (Original work published 1972).

Pitt, B., Gardner, D., Kleiner, J., Wlodkowski, S., Noorani, T(Producers). & Murphy, R (Director). (2010). *Eat, pray, love* (Motion Picture). United States: Plan B Entertainment.

Powell, J. (1969). *Why am I afraid to tell you who I am?* Illinois, USA: Argus Communications.

Runkel, H.E. (2011). *The self-centered marriage: Rebuilding your "we" by reclaiming your "I"*. New York: Three Rivers Press.

Schlitz, M.M, Vieten, C. & Amorok, T. (2007). *Living Deeply: The art & science of transformation in everyday life*. Oakland, CA; New Harbinger Publications.

Sharma, R. (2004). *Discover your destiny: With the monk who sold his ferrari*. Toronto, ON: HarperCollins Publishers Ltd.

Schomer, A., Morrissey, R (Producers). & Noonan, K (Director). (2017). *Heal* (Documentary). USA.

The Greater Good Science Center. (2018). *Greater Good Magazine: Mindfulness Quiz*. Retrieved from https://greatergood.berkeley.edu/quizzes/take_quiz/mindfulness.

Thich Nhat Hanh. (2014). *No mud, no lotus: The art of transforming suffering*. Berkeley, California: Parallax Press.

Tolle, E. (2001). *The power of now: A guide to spiritual enlightenment* (Audiobook). Novato, CA: New World Library Audio.

Tutu, D. & Tutu, M. (2014). *The book of forgiving*. New York, NY: HarperCollins Publishers Ltd.

Two Wolves— A Cherokee parable. (2018). *Pearls of Wisdom*. Retrieved from http://www.sapphyr.net/natam/two-wolves.htm.

Vitale, J., & Hew Len, I. (2007). *Zero limits: The secret Hawaiian system for wealth, health, peace and more*. Hoboken, New Jersey: John Wiley & Sons, Inc.

Walmsley, J. (2017). *Angel numbers—Joanne sacred scribes*. Retrieved from http://sacredscribesangelnumbers.blogspot.ca/p/index-numbers.html.

Welwood, J. (2000). *Toward a psychology of awakening: Buddhism, psychotherapy, and the path of personal and spiritual transformation*. Boulder, Colorado: Shambhala Publications, Inc.

Zukav, G. (2011). *Spiritual partnership: The journey to authentic power*. New York, NY: HarperCollins Publisher.

Acknowledgments

A few years ago, I got a message that popped into my mind that I was meant to write a book. I found it curious because I had never considered myself to be a writer and had no idea what the book would be about. This message came from an intelligent life force that needed to be expressed through me in the right time and in the right way. It came at the beginning of what was about to be a radical transformation in my life. When I came through the transformation and began to understand that it was a necessary journey many women are being called to take, I had an inner knowing of what this book was meant to be about. Perhaps I am most grateful to this mystical life force that is forever seeking expression through each of us.

There have and continue to be many women who have journeyed with me and shared their stories, hearts and Souls along the way. I am continually amazed at how similar we all are even though our life circumstances are often very different. Each one of you has touched me in a deep and lasting way and without you, this book would have not been possible.

My husband Mark, who has journeyed with me since I was 16 years old. Mark lived this unknown and often emotional and uncertain transformation with me. Mark was the first person to read this book and wholeheartedly supported the sharing of a story that often included him. Because of his love, kindness, strength, and the space that he gave me, we have grown closer together and are more deeply connected in both a human and spiritual way.

My daughter, Erika, and my son, Scott, have been my greatest gifts and my teachers. They taught me unconditional love and acceptance, and to let go and trust that there is a higher intelligence at work. They, along with their spouses, Andrea and Conrad, have brought Johnny and Brooklyn into the world. Deep down I wanted to write a book that my grandchildren and their children would read one day. If there is one thing I would want for my grandchildren and all the generations to come after them, it is that they follow the callings of their Soul and in doing so, drown out the voices of others—no matter how well intentioned the voices may be.

I am deeply grateful for my parents who gave me the gift of my own life. My Soul chose them as my parents, and I wouldn't have the amazing life that I have without them. I learned some of life's biggest lessons from them.

My sisters, Nora and Heather, who started as sisters and over the years became my closest friends. We have a special bond and a deep connection that will continue for the rest of our lives, both in this physical world and beyond.

To my extended family and friends who have encouraged, supported and cheered me on when I had doubts about whether I could write and finish this book. Many experiences and countless hours have been shared with my family and closest friends that helped me gain clarity and meaning around the process of transformation and what it means to be an awakening woman.

A special thank-you to my friend Judy, who not only shared her heart and Soul with me, but also the amazing gift of editing this manuscript as it was nearing completion.

To my family who are no longer here in physical form but whose energy and love I feel on a daily basis.

I'm extending heartfelt gratitude to Sarah McLean and the amazing team at the McLean Meditation Institute® for their tireless commitment through training and support to make the world a more peaceful place. They truly opened the door for me to explore practices to awaken my Soul.

Gratitude also to Rev. Pat Campbell, the minister at the Centre for Spiritual Living who has been my spiritual guide and mentor. She and the entire community have stood as a "beacon of spiritual illumination" for me as I ventured into the exploration of what it means to be a spiritual being, having a human experience.

I'm grateful to all the meditation teachers and spiritual guides who have inspired me from afar. To Eckhart Tolle, for planting the seed of hope that life could and was meant to be lived one moment at a time. To the Dalai Lama, who reminds us that kindness and compassion are the way of the spiritual warrior. To Tara Brach and Jack Kornfield for sharing your practices, wisdom, and hearts so freely and compassionately. To Sonia Choquette for the half-hour call that gave me the gentle nudge to begin writing this book. And so many others whose books and wisdom have been highlighted in the pages of this book and imprinted on my heart.

Thank you to all those amazing human beings who have attended one of my workshops or programs in order to bring greater peace into your lives and ultimately into this world. Each one of you has left a mark on my heart and touched my Soul.

And finally, to you the reader who has embarked on this journey with me and many other women, I'm beyond grateful that you have chosen to read this book on your journey of awakening. Every small step towards shifting your life to align with your Soul will create a ripple of healing in this world. Thank you, from the bottom of my heart!

About The Author

Bev Janisch is an advocate for women's Souls. She is on a mission to alleviate the "Soul hunger" and suffering that arises when women's outer lives are not in alignment with their Souls.

Since 2013, Bev has been teaching, coaching and mentoring women who are feeling like something is missing in the midst of living abundant lives. Bev specializes in helping women integrate a variety of meditation, mindfulness and other Soul-expanding practices into their lives in order to shift from surviving to thriving.

Bev's programs and services include tools, wisdom and guidance for women to make Soul-inspired changes. Bev's signature coaching and mentoring program is a four-month journey for women who are ready to experience greater joy, inner peace and fulfillment in all aspects of their lives.

Bev has a master's degree in nursing and worked as a nursing leader for over 30 years. She intended to follow the well-worn path of enjoying her early "retirement," but the universe had other ideas for her. Bev's Soul was summoning her to live a life with deeper meaning. Meditation and mindfulness became the tools that enabled Bev to quiet her mind so that her Soul could speak.

Bev lives in Calgary, Alberta, Canada with her husband, Mark and her dog, Molly.